THE FREEDOM PARENTS

Take Your Family From Struggling and Frustrated to
Fulfilled and Free!

SAMANTHA AND HAROLD LEE PRESTENBACH

Contents

Foreword   v

Acknowledgments   ix

Introduction   xiii

Free Gift   xix

1. Tap Into That Untapped Potential   1

2. Roots   15

3. Grit and Grace   37

4. Side Hustle Hopes   49

5. Fight for Your Future   61

6. Learning to Soar   71

7. Let's Talk Business   81

8. Counting Stars   107

9. Recipe for Success   129

10. The Freedom Frontier   149

11. Call It a COMEBACK   161

12. Manhood, Fatherhood & Fulfillment   171

The Freedom Parent Playlist   191

The #FreedomParentTribe Tells You About Their New American Dream   193

Foreword

I'm very excited for you as I write this foreword! Reading this book and looking back on the life journey of Samantha (Sam) and Harold, I'm compelled to say this to you, the reader . . . CONGRATULATIONS; YOU'VE MADE IT! Really, I mean this for you.

Pause and consider this mind-blowing fact . . . Your entire life, which includes everything you've ever done, every decision you've ever made, and every single thing that has ever happened in all of history and creation, has conspired and prepared you to be in this very moment!

So, hallelujah, yes, when I say congratulations! You made it to right here and right now! I could go into the scientific odds against your very existence of being on this earth, but simply know this, YOU ARE A MIRACLE!

It was 2010 when I spoke at a fitness conference in Costa Mesa, California, and only God knew that two then strangers would grow to become two of the most trusted people in my entire life. Certainly, Harold and Sam had no idea they would learn how to transform every one of their paralyzing pains, problems, and failures into a multimillion dollar Freedom Parent legacy! Honestly, I, "The Mentor" at the time, did not anticipate that I would become their student in just a few short years; soon to be watching and learning from them how to teach other parents, couples, and single people how to create a spectacular life full of happiness, time, and money freedom far beyond what their current minds can believe possible!

I feel it's important for you to know that Sam and Harold are real people just like you. So back to 2010 Costa Mesa, California; I'd just finished my keynote speech. Having pressed her way through a crowd of 400 people tightly packed together, tears running down her face, she touches my arm. Composing herself, she sets her face firm and looks me straight in the eyes, "Hi, I'm Sam," she says with her captivating Louisiana accent. She proceeds, "Alex, your presentation gave me hope . . ." but little did she or I know, she, too, would be a part of my hope and future life's work. Sam went on, "My husband and I need your help in our lives, in our marriage, and in our business." With a look of deep concern, she quickly looks over her shoulder, scans the room, and then places her eyes back on me. Her tears, having now turned into a stream of pain bordering fear. She swiftly placed her business card in my hand while sniffling and gasping for air between words, "I can't let my husband, Harold, see me talking to you with these tears. He would be so mad that I'm telling you this, but Alex, our marriage is a disaster, I'm pregnant with our second child, our business is failing, we fight all the time, and we're on the verge of bankruptcy . . . Alex, like you said in your speech about how it was in your marriage that's now coming to an end after 10 years, Harold and I are living a lie; we pretend like everything is okay, but we're barely holding on . . . Please, call me on my mobile."

She looks to the side and sees her husband making his way through the crowd, then over at me. Her face is now serious and 100% focused. With command, she tells me, "Right now, I need you not to say a word to Harold about what I just told you because he's coming over here, and I can't be crying. He'll be so mad; it won't be good . . ." Seconds later, tears wiped away, and a huge smile on her face, Sam introduced me to Harold Prestenbach.

Readers, friends, and now fellow Freedom Parents Tribe members, if you're not already seeing the possibility for how your life could be blessed and on the verge of a major facelift, heart-lift, and abundant blessing by reading this book and engaging in a relationship with Sam and Harold, then let me now invite you to do just that!

Sam and Harold are here for you now. They have been through the fire, and they know the way through the trials, heartaches, and setbacks. More importantly, they have the heart and the ability to help you rise up and lift your life to a whole-notha-level! Yes, I said "notha," because proper English just doesn't fit the experience you're about to have in your life moving forward as a part of the Freedom Parents Tribe!

PS: Just as I've already met so many people who have followed the proven Freedom Parents path to success, I truly look forward to meeting you and hearing how you, too, are blown away by the levels of breakthrough, growth, and success you've created by choosing to allow yourself to be coached by Sam and Harold!

With love and blessings,

Alex McMillan CEO & Founder

Alex McMillan International and Another Level You

Acknowledgments

Harold: Let's face it, I have practically dedicated this whole book to you. You are my inspiration. When I think I'm crazy, you meet my "crazy" and ante up. You take mediocre dreams and give them their grandeur. I would not ever want to live this life with anyone else. I love you.

Sabella Jane', Mila Joli', Stellan, and our fourth baby (whom we have yet to meet): You are the gift of life and love. There were parts of us, of course, that wanted to live a successful life and have our act together before having kids, but we lacked the conviction. Until you. Then came you, and with that, the meaning of life and love expanded. We learned that to truly love and serve you we had to learn how to truly love and serve ourselves as well as others. You taught us to embrace the struggle as the way to strength. You taught us to fight for what was right and what is right: true freedom. You helped us to dream and you will forever be our most beautiful creation ever.

To our parents, Donald and Gail Jane' and Harold and Diana Prestenbach: Thank YOU! Thank you for loving us, working hard your whole entire life, always doing the best you could, never abandoning us, believing in us, and being the best parents we could ever ask for. We know how much you endured for the love of your children. We know how much it meant to you to elevate us to another level in life. You will always be the real Giants whose shoulders we stood upon, and we will never forget it. We love you.

#TheFreedomParentTribe: our friends, team, colleagues, supporters, mentors; you know, the crazy ones. We share a common thread. We thank you for living your life BIG, for serving your family and others and for trusting that YOU can make a difference in this world. We thank you for receiving our belief in you as well as always believing and trusting us. We love you and are thankful that you are our hand-selected friends with whom we get to live this life with daily.

Elizabeth Heil and Maria Fernandez: Thank you for encouraging me through the final edits and reading the book in the infancy stage. Your words filled me up with confidence and pride in the work that lies in these pages. You are amazing friends and I can't imagine life without you.

Our Closest Mentors: Alex and Jill McMillan, Craig and Anita Blanchette and David and Terri Miller. You saw something in us when we were at the lowest point of our lives. You proclaimed victory, strength, and ability over us to change our stars. You gave us the skills. We love you and thank you daily from the bottom of our hearts.

Lizette Balsdon: Thank you for being the most wonderful first-time experience working with an editor. You were kind to my newbie-writer heart as much as you were patient with me not having the slightest understanding of the writing, editing, and publishing process. You are 100% a professional and turned my manuscript into the art I envisioned.

The amazing Qat Wanders: You are like a Wonder Woman of editors. As freshmen authors, we are so thankful that we now realize how impactful it is to have not just one, but two editors. Having your eye on our work was such a gift. Thank you!

Vito Lafata, Mike Murphy, and the whole Visionary Planner team: Thank you, Vito for reaching out to Harold and encouraging us to dream even bigger. Mike, thank you for putting all the pieces together and helping us turn #TheFreedomParents into a reality.

Self Publishing School: Thank you for providing me with the resources to finally take action on the dream of writing a book.

Introduction

"Resistance told me I shouldn't seek to instruct, or put myself forward as a purveyor of wisdom; that this was vain, egotistical, possibly even corrupt, and that it would work harm to me in the end. That scared me. It made a lot of sense.
What finally convinced me to go ahead was simply that I was so unhappy not going ahead. I was developing symptoms. As soon as I sat down and began, I was okay."
—*Steven Pressfield,* The War of Art

Books about business, direct sales, and network marketing are sometimes boring! Are they helpful, important, and even essential? Yes. But they are often rote and tell you the same thing over and over again. This, I must say, is a good thing. If it wasn't for leaders who emerged from various companies that were bold enough to make the huge leap into educating the entire profession, Harold and I may not be writing this book now. So my hat goes off to you, dear sirs and ladies, for educating and empowering us. But rote strategies, no matter how effective, often go unseen and under-utilized until we discover a reason to put it to use. Until our minds are engaged to see that simple strategies will lead to an incredible life-altering transformation of your very own, let's face it, no one is listening.

Part of the reason so many people don't succeed in this industry is that they undermine just how simple the actions to build a successful business can be. Simple is very different from easy, but if you have done your research, you can back me up here that the techniques—although they might have different terminology from company to company—are very much the same. The next part of that recipe for failure is quite honestly that we lack conviction and passion, or we possess conviction and passion but rather are just not bringing it into a business and the lives we could change. So we have chosen to share our story—one of a broken family on the edge of bankruptcy who found a way to mend and come back stronger, happier, and freer than ever. We are a tribe of chain-breakers.

Who are we to be writing this book? Who are you to crave an enhanced life? Who are you to dream that your dreams might actually still be a reality or that there is a spark designed in you destined to become a fire that changes other people's lives? Who are we to achieve life freedom? Who are we to succeed in network marketing?

When I started writing this book, I had all of these thoughts and then some. Writing a book has been a dream planted in my head since I was in first grade. Being the proud owner of a happy, successful, love-filled, abundant, and adventurous life; a dream planted in me from birth.

So who are we? We are everyday average people just like everyone else, but with an above-average desire to succeed and help others do the same. We, including you, are the people who couldn't silence the calling within us to ask, seek, and knock. Yes, both Harold and I are full-time network marketers. Yes, we have been blessed financially beyond our wildest dreams in this industry. Yes, we had NO idea what we were doing when we started. Now, as a top earner in our company (this is our full-time gig), we have clearly learned how to grow a significant business in the world of direct sales.

However, be advised that this is NOT your average network marketing book, and we are probably not your average top leaders. If you're expecting a check-list of strategic actions, or pages of industry "one-liners" to convince people to join your team, you can close this book now. Yes, there is a time and place for strategy, action, and systems. Without those things, we would not have risen to the top of our industry, and most importantly, we would not have a proven blueprint to guide others to the same course of success and freedom. But there was a major pivotal shift that happened long before we adopted systems and became a business powerhouse. There is a hidden story behind our transformation. This hidden detail is the most important element of the transformation that you are praying for this very moment.

We made heart, head, and home shifts first. We made the decision to leave behind our baggage, become the partners the other deserved in our marriage, life, and business, to become the kind of parents our kids craved and to grow into the leaders that our team and future team deserves. We decided to roll up our sleeves and get to work. We literally grew into more evolved individuals. As we made this shift in ourselves, every single thing got better. It became a wonderful side bonus that our bank account was growing because what was most exciting is we were becoming the kind of people we had always envisioned we would become. And, even more exciting, the people around us were empowered to believe they could do the same.

In this book, we are going to encourage you and empower you to become a victorious person, a responsible person, a driven-by-dreams person and a committed-to-success person. You will become an "It starts with me" person. Because that's just it, no one will ever be more committed to your success than you, and it will take you deciding to step into that reality far before it's actually a reality. It's our greatest desire to bring you the pivotal mind shifts and heart shifts we had during the process all into this one book because in order to have this inspirational breakthrough first, and then to become business leaders, we had to search inside and outside our industry long and hard. We do not want your growth to be delayed by jumping down one rabbit hole to the next. We want to bring you into our family and give all our secrets away so hopefully you can skip some of the hard stuff and just get right to the art of evolving.

You will notice that each chapter begins with a quote from a song. Listen to each song before and after you read that chapter. If you're anything like me, I believe it will allow you to see into this transformation that much more, but also allow you to dream for yourself. If you're not like me, and music just moves your feet but not your soul, just enjoy some good tunes. But do relax and dream. After all, our biggest hope is that you will start to dream again and be inspired into action.

When you read this book, you are automatically adopted into #TheFreedomParentTribe. But what is that, anyway? Well, one thing is certain, we are not a personal brand attempting to extend our own name; we are a people brand.

The Freedom Parent tribe is a mission created out of inspiration that all people who desire to break free of the random 9–5 grind can do so if they choose. This is more than just a story; it is a mission and a template for complete freedom.

A mission to bring wives back to husbands, husbands back to wives, parents back to children and fulfillment, joy and adventure back to all men and women who want it at any age. This is a mission to help you discover *your* American Dream.

Could that be you? If so, you, too, can become a torch-bearer and beacon of hope. That is what the world needs more of; hope. As we have people who are willing to reach down to us, then we must also reach down to others. Are you willing to become the highest version of yourself and turn your dreams into reality so that you can guide other people around you in creating their own transformation? I hope so. I hope you are the one.

Let's all complete the legacy and the circle together. Thank you for joining the mission and welcome to the family.

Free Gift

The Freedom Goal Planner:
www.thefreedomparents.com

Join the community and the conversation at:
Facebook: www.facebook.com/thefreedomparents
Instagram: www.instagram.com/thefreedomparents

ONE

Tap Into That Untapped Potential

"If you could soldier on, headstrong into the storm, I'll be here waiting on the other side. Don't look back the road is long, the first days of the war are gone. Take back your former throne and turn the tide."
NEEDTOBREATHE ~ "Keep your Eyes Open"

I love my husband. Actually, I'm totally *in* love with him; he is my soulmate.

WHOA, Nelly! Hot and heavy in the first chapter, you say? Believe me, I am laughing with you, but there is a point, and I ask that you hear me out.

Side note: I am really smitten with my husband. He is super hand-some, smart, and has a cute tushie! What!? It's true. You should just know right now that this is how I am. Hi! I am Sam, and I will be guiding you through the next 11 chapters of this book. Then, you will reach chapter 12 and talk to Harold. He will be a breath of fresh air, trust me. Until then, this is me telling our story. I am a little dorky, kind, very passionate, feisty, and like to think I am funny and will say just about anything to the point I realize I should insert foot. Are you feeling me? Okay. Good! Let's proceed.

So, why am I telling you this? Because I truly believe the kind of people who believe in such a thing as "soulmates" are exactly the kind of people who think and dream big. Furthermore, I believe people who value love—and I'm not just talking about love between a husband and a wife; I'm talking about love, plain and simple—are some of the most motivated people in the world. They are also some of the most fulfilled. Love makes life worth living. Love makes our work—and the necessary effort we put into it—worthy.

Before we can go any further here, I need you to open your eyes and your heart and start dreaming bigger! Can you do that for yourself? Your goals and your future depend on it. So many people automatically think that in this business, it's all about striving for money and things—or even worse, most people think that succeeding in network marketing is relative to finding a unicorn. It's impossible. But that doesn't keep them from buying their lottery ticket (AKA their distributor's kit). I might have stepped on a few toes just now. I say it because I have done it, so I have been in that club, too.

Many people are okay with losing a little bit of money, just in case success is possible. All the while, they don't actually believe it is and therefore never invest their most important asset: their time and mental energy.

While I want you to have a financial goal for the right reasons, you don't need to start there first. Instead, let's become curious about what else might be missing. When you look at your life and the things or people you love—what about them and your current situation breaks your heart? Those are the things you desire to change.

I believe love is the most important thing in life. It's the most pure form of healing and creation. So I'm going to tell you this story as an analogy, and as I do, I want you to ask yourself, "What goals can I set for myself and my people based in love and creation for the life I desire us to live?" This is assuming that if you knew you could create a better life with more options for yourself and your loved ones, you would.

All right, hang in here with me and picture this. There is this one person who believes beyond a shadow of a doubt that God created one perfect match for him or her in the entire world, which as of 2018, makes up 7.6 billion people. (Oh, how tempting it is to use my best Dr. Evil voice here. I do love a good *Austin Powers* movie.)

Now, that is pretty remarkable when we really stop and think about this concept. I mean, what are the odds that one person can find *their* one person out of all of those people on Earth? The chances are definitely slim, but there is a chance! Slim or not, it doesn't matter because it's totally and completely possible. So what is it, after all, that takes possibility a stretch further and makes it a probability? How do we take a dream from a concept to something concrete? Something we can touch and experience.

Possibilities become probabilities when we combine belief with necessity. You see, for me, true love was not just going to be an unexpected bonus in my life. I didn't sit up at night thinking to myself, "Well, if I find love, it would be so great, and if he happens to stand for all the things I stand for, that would be even better, I guess. If it's possible, that would be nice."

No, no, no! Dang it, I expected love. I expected the kind of love that would make my heart go pitter-patter until the day I die. Does that sound dramatic or unrealistic? Maybe, but you know what? I took finding my soulmate pretty seriously. It was a non-negotiable goal.

I met my husband when I was eighteen, and he was just twenty-two years old. So you can imagine the kind of focus we had to find each other so young. Now we have thirteen amazing years of marriage behind us. He is my best friend.

That doesn't mean that I have never questioned him or his actions, or that he has never questioned mine. It also doesn't mean we have never struggled, fought, or made mistakes. Quite the contrary; we have fought a lot, and we have made a ton of mistakes—more than I can count. But the fact remains; when I kissed that man for the first time in 2001 on a pitch-black summer night, when all the electricity was out after a storm in the sticks of the Louisiana countryside, I saw stars.

I'm not exaggerating. I literally saw stars. What I felt and saw at that moment was 100% real, and I might add, familiar. I felt my forever in his arms, but it wasn't exactly a shock. That moment felt just like I always knew it would. No, it felt like I always *envisioned* it would.

Your Vision is Your Compass

Now, how many times in your life have you felt that strong about something or someone? I have been pretty lost and pretty hopeless many times in my life, but there have always

4

been a few things I was 100% certain I needed: Love, success, legacy, faith, and to be of service to humanity.

I call this my Life Compass. These are the core values and desires that steer me—and probably most of humanity. You see, I decided a long time ago who I was going to be when I grew up:

1. A child of God.
2. A woman pursuing a career that was spiritually and financially fulfilling.
3. A wife in love with the man of her dreams.
4. A mother.
5. A person who could positively impact others.

Simple enough, right?

We all have basic human goals that lay a foundation for everything else we pursue. These foundational goals strike us in random moments. Call it signs, coincidence, basic human needs, or fate . . . Personally, I don't care what you call it; just don't ignore it.

How do you know what your core goals are that will make up your compass? Well, these are the moments that stir you to your core. Moments that make you feel so alive (good or bad) that it often creates quite a mess in the beginning and redefines all your other plans. These are the moments that change the course of your life forever. It is the fork in the road.

It resembles the moment you truly know God and feel Him with you. Having your first acknowledgment that you'll never

ever be alone again, and you'll always be loved . . . That's pretty life-altering, right! And suddenly, you have another direction (core goal) added to your compass . . . forever.

Or the first time you hold your child in your arms, look into their eyes, kiss their cheek, and tell them you love them. Suddenly, you know that you have left your mark of love on another person for the rest of your life and theirs . . . Epic! And now, you have another direction on your compass.

Beautiful, isn't it? But perhaps, it is a series of seemingly small events, decisions, and encounters that add up into a cataclysmic fork in the road. Maybe you get a taste for adventure that brings joy and energy to your life and you just can't shake the feeling.

And, sadly, maybe something devastating happens that rips your heart from your chest, but makes you question everything about your life and how you're spending your days. It's these moments that will jump out in front of you, begging you to take a path that will protect what is most important in *your* life.

There are several situations like this for me, one if which was born from my mother's passing on December 11th, 2012. Another was waking up just a few days after we hit our first big business milestone, to hear that my sister had passed away in her sleep at thirty-six years old, holding another sister's hand as she laid in hospice at only thirty-five years old. Then there was grieving the loss of my brother from a car wreck at thirty-six years old.

But there are moments of joy and peace which have also steered me. My love for travel, nature, and experiencing new adventures. Giving birth to my three children; kissing my future husband for the first time; feeling love from my mother and father. There's learning the value of family, sisters, brothers, and friends and the beauty of having a place to belong in this world while being of service.

There are no rules for how life will intervene and what lessons you will gain, but life will indeed intervene. How you read those signs will be up to you. What stirs your soul?

At the time we begin to harness this power (the power to intentionally create a magnetic pay-it-forward kind of life) and lay out a moral heart compass. Many of us walk around not even knowing we possess this skill. Basic human instincts kick in, and it is up to us to take this to the next level.

Basic instincts such as finding a mate, food, water, shelter, and clothing, are natural drivers that are hard-wired into our brains. We seem to forget that there is something magical in us just waiting to be realized. We dumb down some of the greatest opportunities that will ever cross our path, simply because it came with an unlikely label.

The fact is, I dreamed about the man I would marry long before I met him, and I made NO exceptions for anyone else in my life but him. I knew every detail about this man from what he would look like right down to what he would be like. I knew he would have dark hair, blue eyes, and a strong athletic build. I knew he would be smart, kind, strong, faithful, persevering, determined, funny, gentle, adventurous, and an amazing father and love God with all his heart.

I never ever thought I was asking for too much; I knew I deserved him. And here we are. My husband is one in a billion (one in 7.6 billion, to be exact), but I searched for him high and low because my life's happiness depended on it.

Harold grew into the man I always knew he would

become. He, too, came with an unlikely label. He was a local Louisiana boy. I had taken my vision to the minute details that somehow, the only way for me to find love would be at the age of thirty-six (the age I am now), and that I would definitely meet this love out of state. Boy, I was so right and yet so wrong.

You know what? I'm so glad I was wrong about all the right things. The man of my dreams didn't come to me perfectly polished like a Ken doll; we would become polished over time together. No matter what the goal is, it is likely it, too, will come to you in an unpolished form. It will be up to you to see the diamond in the rough and decide if you are willing to put in the effort to make it shine.

Do You Believe the Odds Are for You or against You?

Did you realize that your dreams are waiting on you? The vision you have for your life, the people for whom YOU can make a positive impact, and the positive circumstances and opportunities which only you can create are in your future.

They all are sitting idle and unrealized until you realize you are needed. That's right. People need you right now to start seeing your future and your future self very clearly. People need you to imagine that you are capable of changing your situation. People need to see transformation in you so that they can see it in themselves.

Yes, I just went there. How can we ever impact other people's worlds if we are not impacting our own? How will we ever change our stars, my friend, if you have forgotten how to shine?

Now, let's travel back to finding that one person out of 7.6 billion people in the world to love for the rest of your life. And, hang with me, because I'm making the point I promised I would.

When you want something so much like falling in love, financial freedom, or adventures, do you think the right first step to turn to what we think is "realistic" and measure up what's "impossible," or do you only laser in on what is absolutely possible?

Let me tell you what's possible: Reaching the TOP of your desired network marketing company is absolutely 100% possible. Achieving financial, location, and time freedom: possible. But (like many others) you are probably wasting your future by only thinking about why it may not be possible.

Be honest with yourself. Do you invest more time into doubting your dreams more than you are driving toward them?

I believe the meaning of life is measured by what is absolutely possible! And that is what this story is about. Our story is about turning possibility into probability. Harold and I learned a whole new industry from the ground up and became top leaders and millionaires while we are both in our thirties. Well, that's not exactly realistic, is it? But it happened. We made it happen because there was a chance. We allowed our compass to steer us from breakdown to breakthrough.

So many of us get into our own heads way too often. We ask ourselves, "Who am I to be great? Who am I to say I can help others? Who am I to ignite a mission?" Sometimes, I find that side of my brain still trying to speak up, and then I just tell it to shut it! And next, I fight those voices with the truth.

9

Here's what I do know without a doubt: I know who we are. We are children of God. We love people, we are #TheFreedomParents, and our story is real. We have struggled; we have nearly given up on everything and everyone. We have been beaten up, and we have been lifted up. And here's what I need from you before I continue to lay my heart on the line for the sake of helping you step over that line to freedom. Are you ready to hear it?

Drop your walls. Please, for the sake of your future freedom, can you just drop your guard? Leave your pain at the door and start dreaming again of the possibilities for your life, for your family, and for the people who will meet you that you might as well set free in the process, too.

And might I add, if you change your life and create freedom in this process (because ultimately, it will be up to you to make the change), make the commitment that you will pay the gift forward. That is what network marketing is really about. That's what life is about.

When you get out, you must go back and get others out. A gift isn't truly a gift until it has been given. And that's why I'm writing this book now. I made a vow to God. I vowed that if we trusted, worked, and became the best versions of ourselves and obtained freedom, that we would share our story and help others.

As you will see when you read further, we were not always this happy and fulfilled. We knew what we wanted at the end of the road, but somehow we kept finding ourselves at forks in the road with no sign or direction of what path to take.

Often, we took side roads that led to trouble—roads which seemed like they would lead to the destination we desired, only to then lead us to a mud pit—stuck again. We tasted financial success (driven only by money) and extreme financial lows. We have seen that we could have our bank account full and our hearts empty. Likewise, we have had our bank account nearly empty and our hearts *full* of love, joy, and hope.

We are now living a prosperous life, more abundant than the initial goals we dreamed of in our early twenties, and we are even happier now that we are completely driven by purpose. Our hearts are full, our bank account overflowing, and our family is thriving. You can have this life, too.

As we grew to the top rank of our network marketing company, gracing that stage meant that God took grace upon us. He allowed us to create what I envisioned years before when we sat at our first convention. I dreamed about reaching the top of the company, and that meant we had to become the best versions of ourselves, and we had to serve others. And that, to me, sounded like the kind of success I was willing to fight and work for; it felt like God's purpose.

Then, we achieved the big goal we had set out to achieve by the time I was thirty-five years old and Harold thirty-nine years old, and I knew for sure that this is God's work. Our mission is now to lead others on the path to creating a fortune that can be measured in their bank accounts, but most importantly, in the love they have for their families, friends, the ones yet to come, and the adventures that will mark the days of their lives.

We are all influencing someone. The little eyes that stare up at us, the eyes of our friends or family that are growing weary of the mundane, or the eyes of strangers seeking a magnetic life they have yet to encounter. We all have eyes gazing upon us, looking to see if we will be the ones to break through the barriers to lend a hand to the next man.

Keep Your Eyes Open

It was the vehicle of a direct sales industry that fully unlocked our potential. Who would have imagined that?! Surely, not us. This was not the path we thought we would ever take. We came to this world having zero experience in the direct sales industry and had several concepts—like many people do—approaching this industry. But what we wanted to chalk up to a scam ended up bringing the most amazing friends, mentors, experiences, and tools into our life.

These tools first sculpted us into true life partners—partners who could do more than just live together, but also partners who could constructively collaborate for the good of our family and of others.

Then, one gift after the next, we were increasingly surprised! In this process, we grew stronger than ever in our faith, our parenting, and all other relationships. And, oh yeah, by the way, it saved us from declaring bankruptcy.

The decay did not just stop in our lives. This opportunity literally created a whole new robust life! I feel as though I'm giving away the whole story here, so let's just say we are now living the life beyond our wildest dreams. This reality was but a blurry dream-form of our vision for our future, yet it was the compass directing our path.

We started with a few very important core goals. Those core goals steered us, stalled us, and ascended us. Now, it is better than a dream come true. Our life is a prayer realized because we built our future upon goals that really mattered. Furthermore, we decided not to leave any of those goals behind. Our greatest desire is that we can light a spark in your heart and soul to unleash your dreams, potential, and if you're exploring direct sales, to create a life of freedom.

We can encourage you to dive fully in and let this opportunity chisel you into the leader others need you to become in your marriage, your household, and then your business.

Where are you aiming your vision? Stop looking down and turn your eyes to the stars. You are here to tap into that potential to start turning the impossible into the possible and the unlikely into the likely.

Don't grow a day older without exploring the potential left in you. Find something into which you can pour that talent and energy. You are too important to sit by idly.

When we were just children, our small bodies housed dreams far grander than us, but as our bodies grew and responsibilities increased, somehow those dreams shrank. I don't think it's a choice any of us should be willing to make. Make today the last day you ever tell your dreams to shrink as you rise back up to realize and exhaust every ounce of potential within you. Because, YOU ARE A TOTAL BEAST!

Things to Ponder

1. Set core goals based on love. Love for yourself, people, adventure, and possibility.
2. Work on your belief. Do you believe you and others

are entitled to more out of life? Whatever that *more* might be for you?

3. Remember: Possibility becomes probability when we combine belief with necessity.

4. Develop your compass: Commit to three to four core non-negotiable life goals now. How will these core goals snowball into a dynamic, dream-fulfilling life?

TWO

Roots

"Maybe together we can get somewhere
Any place is better
Starting from zero got nothing to lose
Maybe we'll make something
Me myself I got nothing to prove"
Fast Car ~ Tracy Chapman

You are not a product of your circumstances. It's time to open your eyes and realize this fundamental truth.

For way too long, I believed the lie that my circumstances determined my life, and I do not want you to waste one more second allowing that belief to hold you back. It's a godawful Chinese finger trap; only we insert our fingers into our ears and press in instead of pulling those fingers out.

"La, la, la, la, la . . . I can't hear you," we whisper to

ourselves, afraid of the uncomfortable truths we might hear and the fact that we might suddenly face a crossroad. Yes, you might just have to decide to change a few things in your life and about yourself.

Ultimately, if we just release instead of keeping it all in, we might finally have the chance to do something incredible. Perhaps we will have the chance to grow into who we were meant to be all along.

You see, so many of us are in a position of blame, shame, or justification. We tell ourselves a myriad of stories like, "If I had more successful parents . . ." "If my parents wouldn't have done it all for me or sheltered me . . ." "If I wasn't poor . . ." "If I had more friends, a more supportive spouse, a different personality, was prettier, smarter, thinner, stronger . . ."

Seriously, the list can go on and on. I know because I've been there. In fact, I carried one of my big boulders—the fact that I could not accept personal responsibility for my short-comings, weaknesses, and failures—for way too long. Yep, it's the truth. I was plum full of excuses! Lots and lots and lots of excuses. And it gets better; I had a super bad attitude as a not-so-sweet cherry on top. I really wanted to believe that because I grew up poor in a family of seven, because my parents didn't go to college, or because they weren't successful entrepreneurs, that I just wasn't equipped to be successful.

I love my parents and I thank them for a lot, but I subcon-sciously blamed them more than I was aware. (Sorry, Momma and Poppa.) This unhealthy mindset and behavior led me to walk the very bumpy, unpaved, winding road called Blame Street. I walked it with my head down, tears running down my face, and white-knuckled fists clenched with anger and frustration. Unfortunately, I found a way to force others on this street with me—always the ones who loved me most—and blamed them for the mishaps in my life. This is the Bermuda Triangle of success; it swallows up your potential.

But if you are going to be successful in your home-based business, here's your first rule: STOP blaming others; STOP blaming yourself, and STOP making excuses. Yes, before you can change your physical circumstances, you will need to simultaneously heal your mental situation.

I'm not going to hold back here, because I regard you as a friend now. True friends will tell it to you as it is, and I know that your future success depends on you understanding this first principle. It did for me. Comfortable or not, a friend will bring you the unbiased truth for the benefit of your growth and likewise, bask in the glory of your success and progress. I'm also not just any friend. I'm a friend with credibility. I'm a friend who has walked this walk and succeeded. I'm a friend who wants to see you experience the freedom I have gained. So you should know this here is probably the most difficult step in achieving growth. Are you ready to hear this?

Yes, my friend, physical, financial, spiritual, mental, and intellectual growth hurts. Furthermore, it's a normal and necessary pain, because if you're not feeling the pain of growth then you're feeling the pain of failing. Right now, you are rooted in some weeds and we need to do some pruning. How do I know? You can probably guess, but I had some roots to deal with once, too. In fact, this was the first freedom I gained: freedom from the past.

There are going to be roots that serve you well. Those roots are in fertile ground that will fuel your growth, and likewise, some roots are rotting underneath you, and those roots need to be pulled up immediately. Here's the tricky part, the rotting roots are often tangled up in the fertile roots, and here's where we must start picking through them one by one. Sometimes, it will feel like you're in a maze that will take you surging back and forth from your present to your future and then to your past and just when you think your brain has explored all the uncomfortable angles of your emotions and experiences—WHAM!—it strikes again.

Like a wedding day you never knew you asked for, this process will take you through "something old, something new, something blue." I know, so far you're not feeling uplifted, or are you? Have you felt the struggle but couldn't put your finger on exactly why you are struggling? Have you had these thoughts, too, and not realized—like I once did not realize—that you can just simply choose not to think these thoughts any longer?

We are the sum of our upbringing and experiences—good and bad—unless we decide otherwise. At some point, we have to make the choice to become aware of the "good" and leave behind the "bad." This is the day you get to decide to truly become your own person. Life has happened, life is happening, and life will happen. To constantly fight it or blame it is just nonsense. No, to fight it is unhappiness. And the roots you need to let go of have turned into mindsets and actions that don't serve you in achieving your goals or in guiding others to reach theirs.

. . .

You are the Sum of Your Repeated Unwavering Efforts and Beliefs

I never thought I was enough. At a staggering 5'1.5" (yes, every half-inch counts) I was not tall enough. I was often teased in school and often called "shrimp." I was so small that my strength never seemed to measure up to the other kids'. I wanted so bad to fit in with the athletes and scholars. But, when I decided to try out for volleyball and could not muster enough strength to hit the ball over the net, I quickly ruled out sports. I also didn't think I was smart enough.

Heck, I didn't even pass kindergarten. I remember going in for my kindergarten assessment before starting my very first year in school. I clearly realized as the teacher asked me to do one task after another that I just couldn't understand the instructions.

"She will most likely struggle, Mrs. Jane`. She's immature for her age." Mrs. Pam, the teacher, told my mother. At that time, I didn't know what this meant, but I didn't have to, because what I felt spoke volumes. I was inadequate, and I would not measure up.

My kindergarten teacher was telling the truth, but going into kindergarten, I already knew that the adult who was supposed to be in my corner did not believe in me.

Fast-forward to the end of my kindergarten year, I had not measured up to go on to first grade with my peers, but instead, would move to a new program called Transition First. This was a program created for children who had grown past kindergarten, but were not quite ready for first grade.

This just about ripped my heart from my chest. I already felt small in stature, and now I felt small in every other sense of the word. And then I met my new teacher. What first felt like the worst thing that could happen to me, suddenly became the best thing ever.

My new teacher saw something in me that, until then, I had only seen in the eyes of my mother and father. She was kind, patient, interested in me, and a great listener. From her patience, I was able to realize that I didn't have an intellectual deficiency, but rather an attention deficiency. Through a minor setback, I had stumbled along someone that understood me and helped me understand myself. Experiencing encouraging words versus limiting words from an adult set me up to believe in myself.

I moved out of Transition First as one of the top students and then reality hit again. First grade was hard and again, my attention deficiency and my tendency to daydream were just so strong. My teacher suggested I be tested for special education classes.

I took the tests again and realized I could not cut a straight line through paper—not even if it had a line to follow. To this day, I wonder how this is a fair assessment for children who need special education. While I'm sure the assessments have advanced over the years, that day is etched into my memory. I, this little seven-year-old girl, was not good enough because I cut a crooked line. Again, my heart ached. How could I work so hard and still be so inadequate? What was wrong with me?

Then, while sitting in my first-grade classroom one morning, I realized yet again that my focus was drifting. For a second, I had an epiphany. What if I could do something about this? What if I could catch myself drifting and pull myself back into focus? What if I took responsibility for my shortcoming and used the awareness to become better?

I knew beyond a doubt that I was capable. Everyone else doubted me, but I *knew* I was smart. I refused to accept the limitations being imposed upon me. That day, I went to my mother, and I begged and pleaded with her to not put me in special education. I told her I just knew I could do better than what I was currently doing. I told her I was certain I did not belong in that class.

She looked at me and—thank God!—she listened to me. Just to be clear, there is nothing wrong with special education; in fact, it's a blessing for so many. But for me, it was an inaccurate assessment. I have ADD—not a learning disability.

From then on, I was a stellar student. My weakness was really my super-power. Maybe I could not focus on multiple things at once, but I could laser in one thing better than most. I chose to become obsessed with becoming an A-student. Rarely did I earn anything less than an A, and as I moved from grade to grade, I eventually became a straight-A student.

My self-belief was unlocked that day, and it would be a memory and an achievement I could build upon and reference for the rest of my life, especially when I chose to play the victim.

Fast forward to 2018, and we were packing our house in Louisiana in preparation for our move to Arizona. One of the last things I packed was memorabilia, and I came across a bag from my parents. I had never looked in it until then. It contained a heavy stack of papers. As I leafed through the documents, they took me on a walk down memory lane. Paper after paper after paper was one certificate and award after another for reaching the highest achievement in every single subject in school all the way up to many awards for "Student of the Year" and top student for our parish and state. Oh! There were even awards for cheerleading. Yes, I found a sport. And just for your information—to all those hardcore jocks out there—cheerleading is totally a sport. Please don't burst my bubble.

There were loving letters from many teachers praising me for my focus and dedication. Instantly, I was overcome by emotion. How could I start my education with so little support, understanding, focus, or ability and grow, only to later work my way to the top of my class?

How? Despite my own insecurities, I decided to prove to myself what was *right* with me. I decided to prove others wrong for the right reasons. I made the decision to say "I can" instead of "I can't." I decided to get into training and believing. Because, if you want to play the victim, there are plenty of people who will let you—they might even encourage you that it's okay not to try and to avoid struggle. But the struggle is what shapes us.

Believing is not enough. If you want to make big things happen in your life, you must believe and get into training. Stop telling yourself you are not capable. Make yourself capable. What have you been viewing as a personal limitation that could actually grow to be a strength?

"Broke is a situation but Poor is a state of mind."
~ *My Roots*

Growing up, I had a lot. I had two brothers and four sisters, two loving parents, a dog, a cat, food on the table, a bed to sleep in, shoes on my feet, and clothes on my back. I had a roof over my head and a mom who sang lullabies at night and talked about God. I had a dad who provided for his family and made a fire to cuddle by in the winter. I had mud to play in, a forest to run in, country roads to fly down with my bike, rivers to swim in, and laughter galore. Raise your hand if you loved being a kid!

I looked upon my mom as the most beautiful and zesty creature I had ever known. My father was the strongest and bravest man alive. I was a rich child. Those were simple times.

It was not until I was in middle school that I began to compare. As I made friends and ventured out my own home, I saw there were some disparities between my home and those of my family and my friends'. That horrible game of comparison that had started for me when I was just five came back with a ferociousness that would consume much of my adolescence and most of my young adult years. Suddenly, instead of just being wrapped in the warmth of all I loved about my life, I became engorged in the coldness of what wasn't right about my life according to the world around me. Until I was in sixth grade, I was pretty certain I had everything I needed in my life.

Sure, I knew that we were not rich in dollar bills y'all. We were definitely far from the life of the rich and famous, but to me, our home was our refuge, our kingdom, and my family was royalty in my eyes. It did not matter that the walls in my house were just unfinished sheetrock or that the floors were just boards or laminate floor tiles. I didn't mind the cockroaches. My siblings and I used to laugh when we would turn on the lights at night and they would scatter. It was a game. It wasn't until I saw my parents consumed by the stress of terminating the vermin that I realized it was a problem.

Truth be told, in the area in which we grew up, most people lived in trailers or pretty small, old houses. We were fortunate to have the home we had in the first place. It was a home built by father's own hands and left unfinished so he could put food on the table. We made mud pies, caught crawfish in the ditch, rode our bikes, ran barefoot, and climbed trees to our hearts' delight.

In the winter, the home was very drafty; the cold air seeped right through our unfinished walls. My dad would chop firewood for the wood-burning stove, and my mom would put us in thermal, footed pajamas, wrap us in layers of blankets, and make hot cocoa. I loved the smell of fresh chopped wood turning into smoke and ash drifting among the house. It was cozy. My life was a dream.

Sure, when it snowed occasionally, I noticed that my parents' emotions and mine did not match up. I was ecstatic; it was a snow day!!! My parents, on the other hand, were frantic and fearful. They could lose electricity or not have enough wood to keep us warm, so they draped us in layers and layers of blankets at night. For the children, it was just pure fun, but for my parents, it was life or death. Their stress made no sense to me. All I saw was glorious snow angels and elaborate snowball fights. My winter wonderland was their winter nightmare.

In the following years, the pieces of the puzzle began to fall apart slowly. Eventually, one of the first dysfunctions in our family became apparent. There was not enough money for my parents to truly give us what they wanted. We had what we needed most of the time. But then there were pivotal moments that make a child wake up from his or her daydreaming. Their fiery effort to eradicate the roaches was one. My parents budgeting to afford cheerleader uniforms for my sister and me. And, standing in line for government assistance with my mother was another one of those moments.

At first, I just thought it was cool! I was going to get to eat that cool soft cheese everyone loves so much and drink grape juice! We never had juice—just water, milk, or sweet iced tea. I remember being so excited that I couldn't wait to rip into that generic block of Velveeta cheese. As my mother watched me pour myself grape juice, she began to cry. I knew instantly that she was exhausted, worried, and feeling defeated. Yet, despite her despair, her child was happy. She smiled and then cried again. Her words bring me chills even today. She sobbed, "I had to get food stamps to give you juice and cheese."

These are the moments that break you first, and then they make you. Like the time the whole family went to Walmart. We never went to Walmart as a family. Too many kids, too many desires, too exhausting, and too little money.

However, on this occasion, we needed hiking boots for our yearly summer vacation. I know, you're thinking, "Yearly vacation, hmmm . . . You couldn't have been that bad off!"

My dad worked all year long to get one or two weeks off. All year long, my parents saved and planned for our camping trip. Visiting the National Parks was often free or charged minimal fees, and my parents slowly bought and stored our camping gear year after year.

That was the year I received my official hiking boots! It was a badge of honor. They were pink and, I can imagine, tiny. I remember the loving look on my parents' faces when they picked up those boots. I can only recognize it still because I imagine the same look is on my face today when I pick up tiny, cute clothes for one of my babies. My parents were as excited to buy those boots for me as I was to receive them.

As we wheeled off with our buggy, one more thing caught my eye. I honestly don't remember what the toy was, but of course, I needed it right then and there—you know how kids are. I'm sure you can imagine the constant, dramatic begging. And I begged like crazy until my dad broke.

"NO!" he belted out and then paused as he quietly continued with tears in his eyes and his head hung low. "We don't have enough money. I want to give you everything, but I just can't."

Seeing my father feel so defeated lifted a veil from my naïve eyes. My hero had a wound. And I, his child, was the only one who could make it bleed. We all walked away from the store that day with a much different attitude than the one with which we entered. We walked away sad.

My parents were sad because they probably felt as though they were falling short, and I was sad that I had discovered my two heroes had wounds. Their greatest goal and dream was to have a large family. My parents succeeded; they had seven children. The rewards for that dream realized was grand but so were the responsibilities that came along.

I learned a lot from my parents. They worked harder than

most people I know. My father worked either two weeks on and two weeks off, or one week on and one week off on an oil rig offshore in the Gulf. It was a hard life for both of my parents, but it was an occupation I believe my father enjoyed, and it also provided for their family.

My mother was a part-time single parent. This took a heavy toll on her physically and mentally. It also made it difficult for my father to parent when he spent half the year not knowing what was going on at home without him. In my older sister's teenage years, the toll of this divide for the sake of earning money would show up in my sister's rebellious nature and poor choices. While my mother had several babies on her hip to chase, it made it really difficult to chase teenagers at the same time.

My parents were looking for ways to break free. My mother was very creative and thought up several entrepreneurial ventures and my father knew the importance of building wealth. They were never okay with struggling to get by. Had they had the opportunities, the technology, the support, and the community we have today, they would have experienced tremendous success. But they didn't. It's not that they didn't try.

My poppa, I'm going to call him that now, because that's what I call my dad, was introduced to Amway around 1987. And it would be our family's first and last experience with network marketing.

My father started off with excitement and hope. In fact, I had never seen him so alive. He was intrigued by the concept of residual income, and being familiar with hard work, it made sense to him to invest time and effort in growing something that would eventually create new life and financial freedom. Unlike his current career, which kept him away from his family and had us living paycheck to paycheck, he figured it was worth a good shot.

Being a leader in the industry now, I can tell you firsthand that my father put more time and energy into his new business then than most new partners I see joining the industry now. He sat the whole family down and painted a picture for us as to what this business could do for our whole family.

"We could be millionaires," he said. Not quite sure what that meant, I asked him, "Does that mean I can have my own room and a pony?"

"Honey, you can have anything you wish," he replied.

Knowing what desperation looks like on my father's face, seeing hope on his face sure was exciting. That same night, he would ask us all for our help. It meant he would need us as a practice audience while he perfected his presentation of the business opportunity. It would mean us going to his mentor's house so he could learn more from him. And it would mean his occasionally being gone while he was home for his one or two weeks off.

As a child, the presentations lacked the Disney effect—as you can imagine! My mom would pull us aside prior and threaten us—insisting we had to stay awake and behave.

To be completely transparent here, numbers and compensation plans are not my gig—that's Harold's department. Even now, I am good with just knowing the basics while mentoring our coaches, and watching the deposits go into our checking account is super fun, too, but I digress.

So staying awake during a compensation plan presentation

when I was little was difficult! But I did it for my dad. I did because I saw that this man, who was already breaking his back for us to live, was now breaking his back for us to soar. And I loved seeing him excited.

My parents went to two events. One without us, which—for a family of nine—you can imagine is like an act of congress. We hear people all day long make excuses about why they can't attend their company events. Childcare, by far, is the most common excuse. My parents had my aunt, who lived a state away, come in to help. I didn't want my parents to go, but to this day, that visit with my Aunt Glenda was the best!

We made Jello cut-outs and then ate them! It was epic. So many people have guilt about leaving their children for a weekend to chase their dreams. I tell you what, if anything, my parents deserved a weekend away. I ain't sweatin' it—nor should you.

They took the whole family to the next event. Now remember, money was a limited resource, and this was a big deal. We stayed in a legit hotel! I'm not talking about Motel 6 where they keep the lights on. I'm talking about the Fontainebleau Hotel in Miami where the lights shine like it's 1969. Okay, I just like how that sounded.

This was our first-hand experience in the world of the rich and famous. Everything was gorgeous! There were shiny metals, shiny marble, shiny things to buy, and shiny people. Oh my word, guys! This girl has always loved a good sparkle.

Although we spent most of that trip holed up in the room watching TV and eating store-bought eclairs with our older sisters, on the last day, our parents took us to the pool. I'm guessing now that it was a sort of "school by the pool." The people there looked different. They looked successful; they looked as though they were having fun and enjoying life.

I was intrigued and noticed that my father was growing increasingly intrigued. He moved around the pool absorbing wisdom from one leader to the next. He leaned in, he laughed, and he asked questions.

Something about that impressed me even then. My dad is charismatic!?

You would think this is the part where I tell you I am the daughter of a millionaire Amway distributor, right? Sorry, here is where I let you down gently. My father never made it to the top of the company, nor did he even earn a steady income. Maybe this is why I chased the life that network marketing could provide through different avenues. Maybe my father's disappointment in himself turned into disbelief in the company and then to the industry as a whole. Maybe someone in the industry disappointed him. Maybe that company was not the right fit for him. Still, that experience alone was enough to intrigue me and build my curiosity about entrepreneurship. The legacy my father dreamed of achieving eventually came to life in me.

I knew, from this one experience, that I wanted to live a life of creative, energetic abundance and freedom, and gosh darn it, I wanted to love life! For the sake of my children. If we dare to dream of our children truly enjoying the life we can provide them; whether it's making mud-pies in the country or exploring the world, we as their parents need to be free and in love with our life. Poor, middle-class, or rich; if we are not happy, our children will notice. So why not get busy getting happy now?

Now let me rewind. Had my father had the Internet (which didn't exist then), social media (which didn't exist then), virtual teaching platforms that bring you education anytime from anywhere (didn't exist then), a supportive community to learn from (in the sticks, you can say that didn't exist), and access to the higher-ups more frequently (again, thanks to technology), he would have started earning money. And if he could've earned even enough money to pay a bill, he probably would've kept going, and then he would've been able to piece one goal together after another. But he didn't have those things, and lastly, I'll fill in the final piece to the puzzle: he also didn't have my mother's full support. With the resources we have today, there is NO reason not to succeed in the home-based business of your choice.

There you have it, that's certainly not all the pruning, but with that came the good. The roots I kept was, again, love, learning, and the ability to dream. The ability to create the life I want to live in the future. The roots I left behind were the labels and the defeat. I love my family too much to see them suffer, and too much to repeat that suffering. NOW is the best time to improve your quality of life because we just do not know what tomorrow will bring. Now is the perfect time to decide what you will take with you on this journey and what will you let go.

This is not a battle over who is carrying the heaviest boulders in their lives. We are not here to argue that the pain you or I experience is any greater, harder, or more difficult to overcome than another's. Rather, we need to acknowledge these boulders do exist. Sometimes we bring the weight of the past into our future and allow it to hold us down. These boulders are difficult for any one person to carry on his or her own. They cause pain or frustration.

You can't lift a boulder or make it vanish, but you can climb to its peak from where you can see a brighter future on the horizon. Sometimes we can turn our greatest pains into our greatest motivators.

Here's the bottom line, our parents busted their butts to let us live an elevated life—from a higher level than they had previously known. My dad worked his way up from offshore electrician to an office job at ExxonMobil.

My mom made jewelry, became a Reiki master and an ordained minister. Harold's dad worked his way up in construction, and his mom built an income from starting as a teacher at a daycare until eventually, she was the director. They all did this with little more than a high-school education, a lot of drive, and pure passion to give their children a better life. And they did. Can we pause right now and give your parents a big round of applause for doing the best they could with what life handed them? Then accept that you can be thankful for your childhood while still setting out to take that life up another level.

At no point did our parents decide that they weren't worthy of being participants in a better life. They never thought that the better life is only available to the youth. No, they did what they had to do and achieved great things to give their children a better life. They carried their children up another level on the ladder. A few steps closer to a more comfortable family lifestyle than the previous generation is simple and can be done with a little hard work and heart. Creating *massive* family lifestyle breakthrough takes a little bit of crazy and every ounce of strength you have not to give up. Massive breakthrough and lifestyle upgrades are not normal, hence, why you don't see every family living the life of their dreams.

Today, we are direct descendants of pure-grade, 110% heart and hustle. And we must all commit to elevate our children and their children at the very least to the next level in honor of our family heritage.

For a second, imagine your biggest boulders that are holding you back. Identify the roots underneath that you *allow* to hold you back. See it as the giant that it is in your mind. What mindsets and feelings have you allowed to become habits that prevent you from growing or helping others grow? What has stopped you from uncovering your competence and confidence to create a new way of life for yourself?

Let me condense what I discovered to be my biggest boulders and how I pruned through infertile roots to keep the thriving roots:

- Learning difficulties.
- Low self-esteem.
- Poverty.
- Seeing loved ones fail or suffer.
- An overwhelming fear of failure.

In my mind, there was enough evidence that I was not smart enough, pretty enough, strong enough, or important enough to stand out in this world. If you look at all of my insecurities, setbacks, and my (at times) difficult upbringing, you will see that I had just as much a chance to fail as I did to succeed. If history repeats itself, then I should have fallen short of my goals. But I didn't fail despite lots of stumbling. Instead, I looked up at my mountain, released the roots that were grounding me, and I climbed that sucker.

You, too, can look at your past and strengthen yourself in the right ways. Carry that torch and find a way to shine even brighter than anyone in your generation has ever seen. You alone cannot move the mountain, but you can climb it. If you can climb the mountain, then you can conquer the mountain. But first, you must take one step toward the peak.

Look at your setbacks and find the power through the pain. Find the love. Discover how you want to reinstate hope, healing, and the blessing of a future to your family. Stand up and believe you are not the sum of your mistakes or shortcomings —or anyone else's either—but rather, you are triumphant because you persist and shine despite the many pains in your life.

You, my friend, are a *titan*. You are the wounded who refused to be labeled "broken." You have a shield around you, and the arrows that fly at you just bounce off, without causing any harm. You will empower other people to refuse to be labeled broken, and when they're down, you'll show them they *can* go up. You'll demonstrate with your life that when you hit the breakdown, it means there's only one direction left to go: straight up to the breakthrough.

Things to Ponder

1. Ownership: How often do you find yourself on Blame Street?
2. Victorious: Recall a time in your life when you could easily have chosen to play the "victim" card, but instead, chose to step into victory.
3. Resolve: There are moments in our lives that often break us first before they make us better, what defining moments in your life called you to choose a different path?
4. Intrigue: Are you curious enough about what's on the other side of your mountain to release some roots and start trying to climb?

THREE

Grit and Grace

"How we got into this mess, is it God's test?
Someone help us, 'cause we're doing our best.
Trying to make it work but man these times are hard…"
For the First Time ~ The Script

What happens when you have a vision that is vastly different to your current life? Here's the cold, hard reality. You, my friend, are probably reading this right now from a standpoint of *not* being exactly where you want to be in life. And your life might be extremely hard right now. Your feet might hurt, your body may be tired, and your fire might feel like it's almost out, because, in the good Lord's name, things just have not gone as you planned.

Having a plan for your life is pretty important, but have

you ever stopped to ask yourself this very important question: "Am I living my plan, or did I default at some point?"

Let me be the first to raise my hand here and admit that I defaulted. This default plan was so sneaky that I didn't even know it wasn't the right plan until everything around me started falling apart. Switching my trajectory from medical school to entrepreneurship seemed to be the perfect plan, and at first, everything felt so exciting. Once the excitement wore down, it was not long before reality set in. I couldn't imagine that, one day, I would have to decide which one would be worth saving on that happy day when we signed our marriage certificate and business loan.

Before I knew it, everything I'd ever dreamed of started breaking down—not in one collapsed heap, but rather one small bit at a time. Parts of me, my family, my marriage, and my business just slowly broke down and fell away. Between the age of twenty-three and twenty-six, I had actually already accomplished three of my major life goals; 1) marry the man of my dreams, 2) give birth to a beautiful healthy baby girl, and 3) open my own business. But they came with extra company; extras that were completely uninvited and yet there they stood at my front door. No matter how much I refused to look at these uninvited guests, and no matter how much I ignored them, they still showed up day after day.

On a beautiful spring day, my husband and I found our fingers pointed at each other, our words like daggers shooting into each other's hearts. The D-word (divorce) reverberated down our spines, but it seemed to be our only option for a better life apart from each other.

The next of the uninvited guests was a business close to

financial ruin. That's how we uncovered the unwanted gift of family dysfunction. This legacy had been handed down generation after generation and showed up in our marriage. The huge pressure of financial stress was bringing out the ugliest sides of us.

When we thought things couldn't get worse, we had to deal with death as well. We lost so many people we loved and cherished.

I had pictured so many wonderful things in my life, but I never pictured actually achieving many of them, only to see my life in ruins, nonetheless. That wasn't part of my vision. That was *not* my American dream! So here we were; nearly broke, heart-broken, and then I was afraid to announce I was pregnant with our second child. BUT, at least we had a marriage, a family, and a business, right? At least on the outside, we looked like we had it all. As far as anyone else knew, we were happy and successful. However, on the inside, our life was a scream of quiet despair begging for something to save us.

I felt hopeless. I was exhausted. There was love left in our marriage, but we had fought this fight for so long. Just when we were both near ready to just give up on each other; just when I truly thought my husband was a lost cause and there was no hope of him changing so that we could be together; I heard four words, "It starts with you."

The fighting was still going on around me, and my husband was still angry and just as confused as I was, but somehow everything slowed down for a moment as if time froze. I looked at his angry face and saw that it was fear. I knew I couldn't change him because the honest truth was that I hadn't even tried to change me.

Yes, I realized finally that the only person I could save at that moment was me. Was I ready to look in the mirror and see that I was also causing dysfunction in our life? At that point, I had no other option but to become the best version of myself in order to create peace and joy in my home. And if I could find peace and joy, then I can find purpose. And if I could find all these things just because I was given this one life and one chance to make the most of it while having no other hidden agendas to manipulate the situation around me, then maybe I could actually have peace with whatever happens in my life during that process, too. Honestly, I wasn't sure that our marriage could be saved. I wanted it to be saved. I just figured that if my husband was to see the positive changes in me and decided to come along for the journey, then, indeed, we were meant to be together. On the other side, the question gnawed at me: What if he didn't? I had made peace with that choice, because at that moment, the only thing that mattered was peace.

Harold walked away from that fight for a moment. When he returned to me a few minutes later, he said, "I bought us tickets for a business conference and we leave in two weeks to go to California to see how we can save this business. That's if you still want to do that?"

Quite honestly, what went through my head was this, "We can barely live with each other, and you want to save our business? We need to save *us*."

I wanted marriage counseling, but that was my pain. I remembered that I decided the first thing I needed to save was me, and the best version of me would have been to set aside my pain to take a look at the person I love to see his pain over mine.

Harold was suffering. His pain was rooted in that he had left one career of torment to leap into another fire pit. He was drowning. He needed to break out of this financial despair. And finally, I heard the truth: he needed my help. I needed to stop fighting *with* my husband and start fighting *for* my husband.

We fought a lot, but on that day, I finally heard my husband's call. I chose him. I decided I was worth saving, my children's future was worth saving, and my marriage was worth saving. If resurrecting our business was a path to saving those things, then I was willing to fight that fight, too.

We boarded that plane. Because of that choice, we met a stranger (our friend Alex) who would give us our life raft in the form of a home-based business opportunity. A trip that was meant to save our small business would actually give us a completely new opportunity that would do more than simply "save us." That trip would be the beginning of redemption. Before we would take action on that new opportunity, we would continue to pour a lot of money, time, and emotions into trying to save the seemingly unsalvageable, because it was not time to walk away just yet.

"Something's in the air tonight, the sky's alive with a burning light. You can mark my words something's about to break."

Mat Kearney ~ Nothing Left to Lose

Wee Little Lamb, You Are Also a LION

Are you living your American Dream? It was the worst argument of my life that opened the door for healing. When I was at the lowest point of my life and nothing seemed to make sense, I was finally able to see that what I needed most was a fresh start—in every way. I was a hopeless mess at a total rock bottom, but that's where I found answers.

How often do we bring old baggage into our hopes, dreams, and relationships? We cling to this decay as though it will magically turn into a rose with zero remnants of an ugly past. But, what's worse, is that we sometimes think we can just stand still with our arms folded and frowns on our foreheads while we wait for the situation around us to just change on its own. If you are doing this in *any* area of your life, I can guarantee you that you are most likely bringing this bad habit into your relationships or marriage, too.

Let me be very clear here, just in case someone has told you differently; love is work, success is work, parenting is work, and achieving freedom is—most certainly—work. All those things are worth the work.

Do you want to leave this world with a broken heart full of unresolved potential, or a strong heart that has won the right battles? On any given day, I would much rather run into the battlefield than hold the white flag as a spectator in my own life. And if you are deciding that you are unwilling to live a life of regret, then you can no longer play the victim. Not now and not ever again can you blame someone or something for the fact that you are living less than your best life.

Things were dying around us. Some of those things needed to be saved, and they couldn't get the resuscitation they needed because we were distracted by trying to keep other things alive that were beyond our power to revive. We were holding onto baggage that was clearly keeping us from moving forward, but at that moment, when we both let go, we received our fresh start.

Sometimes you don't need to keep reliving the same day over and over. You need to live a new day. If you have a future, you are hell-bent on creating, you better let go of your baggage, too, and step into today's new version of the best you. Stop bringing your old self to your new day—he or she is uninvited.

Do you crave a fresh start? Then you must start looking at the areas of your life to which you must submit. What fights are you fighting long after you should have put your fists down and become meek like a little lamb instead? Are you constantly arguing with your spouse about who's doing the dishes, who will put the kids to bed, who will listen to that training call for your new business venture, or if it's necessary to take that date night or business trip? Listen up; you're fighting the wrong things and the wrong person. That argument doesn't matter.

Stop fighting the one person who loves you at your worst and your best. You should not be fighting *with* your spouse; you should be fighting *for* your spouse.

Lay down, little lamb, and please just try to remember that life partnership is rarely a 50/50 equal opportunity. When our coach, Alex, told me, point blank, that I needed to submit to my husband—I wanted to reach through the phone and punch him in the face. I had just finished telling him that my husband was being a crappy husband at the time. How could he suggest that my husband deserved my submission!?

My disgust at this suggestion proved I did not understand love, relationships, or the definition of submitting in either. Life partners are here for each other at all costs—we supplement one another when necessary. When my husband only has 20% to give, I give 80%. When I had only 10% to give (because there were times I truly couldn't give much), Harold gave 90% of himself. It was because I loved my husband through his flaws and into his strengths that today, I have a life partner and business partner who can love and respect me for my strengths and my flaws—not despite my flaws. If my husband was ever in a place where he could not love me at his best; it did not mean that I could not love him at my best.

This type of partnership doesn't just happen; you have to work on making it happen daily and in every opportunity presented to you. It has meant that there were times I brought him his plate of food and successfully resisted the urge to spit in it because I was so mad at him (true story). That was my victory that day. Seriously, I really did have to resist that urge once, and it makes for a funny memory now—but gosh! Those times were not fun.

Likewise, putting this work in has also meant that I had to be the one on our company calls, and being consistent with the early growth of our #sidehustle which was going to set us free, even though I was tired and wanted to sit down and watch TV, too. Because he spent his 100% at our other business, and I had a little fight left in me at the end of the day, thanks to him.

And there were even the occasions that I just didn't want to be on another call. I just wanted to ride in the car and listen to music. But my husband—who so often stressed about our finances—was interested in learning how to grow this side hustle, and so I bit my lip and listened because it was literally the one thing that gave him hope.

A funny thing happens when we forget about our "feelings" and our "desires" to then decide to do the right thing; we actually grow. You might even learn something, as we both did every time we did something we didn't feel like doing.

Making the decision to step up to the plate and doing what you have to, turns you from a lamb into a lion. You release the pent-up energy you were wasting on unnecessary arguments and turn it into fierce focus. Your roar is created in the way you are actually becoming a new person with a fresh start by putting in the daily action to create the traction that will one day launch a rocket ship. Your steadfast and unwavering belief and vision that you are capable and willing to be that force to break your family free, makes you a force to be reckoned with in a world where most people just give up in the face of anticipation of that kind of work.

You are as much gentle, kind, and understanding as you are a fierce warrior of the light! Merging these two contrasts will help you soar every day. Where you once felt your feet cemented to ground, and the tide was coming in just above your chin, you are now feeling the fresh air swoop under you, lift you up above the wreckage.

Our baggage never just goes away, but here's the beauty: even though it will never just disappear; out of it can grow a rose. The mess is always still there, but out of that mess beauty can prevail. You can turn into a beautiful story of triumph and victory. If you can do that, then you can shine to others who are not that different from you and are also searching for a story of hope.

Don't submit to a default plan for your life just because it was subliminally hardwired into your brain from youth. Don't stay in a default plan just because you think you have no other options, or because you're afraid of what people will think of you for taking a different course. Grow a backbone! Remember, you are fierce!

People's opinions will never pay your bills. People's opinions of you will never write a happy ending to *your* story. Other people only know the desires of their heart. Will you rely on others to write your happy ending or will you pick up your pen and write it yourself? Fight *that* fight, my friend, because that's the fight that really matters. You keeping your eye on you and the things you need to save. Only you can say that you're not happy and that you're choosing to embark on a path to happiness and freedom. If you don't like the way your life is going, then change it. Change it now or stop complaining.

With a whole lot of grit to correct the things most people deem uncorrectable, you can bring grace into your life. Grit brings grace, which in turn brings growth.

It starts with you. Where will you raise your fists, and where will you drop them? When you think about the start of your new beginning, who will be given the permission to shine in their flaws and strengths because today, you made the decision to save you?

"You intended to harm me, but God intended it for good to accomplish what is now being done, the saving of many lives."
Genesis 50:20

Things to Ponder

1. Driver's Seat: Where did you unknowingly default?
2. The Rescue: Who or what is worth saving?
3. Remember: Stop bringing your old self to your new day.
4. #ItStartsWithYou: How can you be a better leader in your household so you can be a better leader in the future? Where will you say "It starts with me," today?

#GRITANDGRACE

FOUR

Side Hustle Hopes

"So this is what you meant, when you said that you were spent. And now it's time to build from the bottom of the pit, right to the top, don't hold back. Packing my bags and giving the Academy a rain check."
It's Time ~ Imagine Dragons

"I don't know if I can do it." I have heard these eight simple words over and over again. I have heard them in my own head more times than I can tell you. And then I hear this from all our partners in one way or another. Either there are the ones who are brave enough to verbally admit their limiting beliefs about themselves and their ability to create the life they desire to live, or I hear it reverberate through people's actions.

You can see and smell a lack of confidence. When you have worked through your own fears and discomforts, this sort of thing is simple to detect. Though it may be simple to detect, it certainly isn't always simple to eliminate.

I have personally met so many people who possessed so much potential, intelligence, and ability to be successful. They have all the connections to drive their success. What I saw in these people was the ability to mold all of their dreams into reality, and furthermore, to help many others do the same. Yet sadly, so many bright people give up. They don't see in themselves what I see.

The sadness I have for these people today—knowing what could've been theirs just a few years later had they just pushed through, had they trusted, had they silenced the voices inside and out—makes me truly feel a loss for them. Furthermore, I grieve for the lives they could have changed that may never have their opportunity, because the person that could have offered it to them, just simply became his or her own obstacle.

We all experience this obstacle. You have heard it said that we are our own worst enemy. Self-defeat is not uncommon. In fact, the first two years of our business consisted of us personally winning the battle of "me against me." What makes us different? Although we and our successful partners may be "different" in your eyes, I can put your mind at ease when I tell you that we are no more special than anyone else.

As I said, the hardest part is what we talked about in the first three chapters. The rest of this is simply putting together a few more pieces to the puzzle, consistently and relentlessly. There are some simple steps anyone can take to overcome the negativity in your own head.

· · ·

I Am Not a Leader (Re-program)

We rode a short fun wave early in our network marketing career. Getting started seemed easy enough. Our first business-building objective was simply to help five people choose health. We purchased our business kit and our own health kit in one day. The next, we texted five people we knew trusted us and were frustrated with not reaching their goals. They started right away, and I noticed the freedom we all experienced.

I had personally reached goals in just a few weeks that, in the past, even with all my experience in the fitness industry, I would have to work for months to obtain. My first clients were all incredible successes, ranging from 30–150-pound losses in record times. We hosted our first event, and several more people signed up. I went from clocking in at our brick-and-mortar business to generate income, to literally getting paid for texting or calling people. Holy moly! I was working from my phone in a matter of days from purchasing my business kit and actually getting paid for it?!

My mind was blown. I had secretly desired this for years since having our first child. I had plotted several ways in which I thought I could earn money working from home—by writing ebooks, creating custom meal plans, and vlogging workouts on YouTube—but all of it would take a lot of time, research, and creation with little to no promise of income. But the vehicle I least expected was suddenly the fastest producing and showed the most promise.

Yet I was stubborn and disrespectful. Despite the incredible successes, the extra income, and the flexibility; I was still not convinced. Imagine that! I believed that if it was meant to be, it was up to me—and only me. I would need to create our path for financial freedom from the ground up, and I would be responsible for duplicating it into a giant. I was also convinced that this was more comfortable. Any other way would be too good to be true.

I knew how to lead me. I didn't know how to lead others. Though Harold saw the potential right away and knew that this business model would—and could—far exceed anything we could create on our own; I would not even listen to him. For the next twenty-four months, I would go through cruise control in our whole life until the breakthrough I needed faced us head on.

It was our company's national convention. We had told our business coach that we would be going. But as it neared, our true intentions definitely surfaced. The phone rang, and my excited business coach began to spout out the details on how to register, and I immediately interrupted him, "Oh, I'm sorry, but we just went on vacation, and we just really can't leave the kids. We won't be able to go." I told him.

I felt at peace with this, or so I thought. After all, to be honest, I really didn't want to go. But it wasn't until my coach did the best thing he could ever have done for us that I realized I would be making a comfortable mistake, but not a good decision. He did not accept my decline. He challenged me. "You told me you would go. Do you still want this? I will talk to Harold if you really want to go," he replied.

Oh, dear Lord. Talk to Harold? I threw him under the bus because I didn't want to go. The truth was I didn't even talk to Harold about it. I assumed he didn't want to go, therefore I would not have to attend either. I had no choice but to tell the truth.

"I'm sorry. I didn't talk to Harold about it. I'm not sure I want to go," I told him.

"Okay, why is that?" he replied.

"Because, Alex, I'm afraid if I go, I will actually have to do this. And I don't know if I can. I am not a leader."

The hard, scary truth. I did not believe in myself. I was afraid of the work involved, and I was afraid I was unworthy to lead others. In my head, I was already a failure. What I did, anyone could do. Anyone could offer a few people health and then just casually text them or call them here and there. But to be the kind of person that leads hundreds to thousands of people to health and then to teach others to do the same—I was not that girl, okay? I took care of me and what was right in front of me, and that was all I knew.

Our coach, Alex, had a true gift: peace, patience, and perspective. He spoke to our hearts and not our heads. He reminded me of what I wanted most. He reminded me of my painful moments. He reminded me of the night I vowed to my infant daughter—with tears streaming down my face—that Lord willing, I would find a way to work from home to be with her. He reminded me that I couldn't stand leaving my children at a daycare and missing their most special moments during the day. Tired, zapped parents. That is what was left of me and my husband at the end of the day when our daughters returned from daycare.

As I got out of my head and back into my heart, I became curious again. My way was not working and my way was wasting our precious time. What if? What if there was a better, faster way? What if this could mold us into people we could be proud of and people our children would be proud of? What if we could become leaders?

"Okay, Alex, call Harold."

Did we go to that event? Yes! Did it change our life forever? YES! Forever and ever in the most amazing ways. It was the first stepping stone of many to transform us into #freedomparents.

Think Small to Get Big

You see, you think too much. *We* think too much. Our silly but powerful brains get a hold of us and throw us around as though we were mere rag dolls.

Worse yet, we allow it. We encourage it, and we celebrate the battery. We become caught up in the tangles of our brains so much that we confuse and overwhelm ourselves with all the possibilities, the "what ifs." But I'm going to tell you now, that "what if?" is enough to start a revolution in your life.

What if *you* are capable of more than you can currently imagine?

Magic happens when your head and heart connect. That magical moment is pure curiosity about the possibility and probability of transformation in your life. The beauty of network marketing is that you *can* lead with your heart into practical next steps. Every company has them. Every leader teaches them. Anyone who has ever duplicated himself or herself and their success in others, uses duplicable, simple systems and steps.

You're worrying about simple things which you do not

need to worry about. Your mentor knows how to help you reach your next milestone. Furthermore, I encourage you to only focus on the one to two most important actions they have put in front of you. If you find yourself unclear on what that is, simply avoid becoming discouraged and seek clarity from your mentors.

Undoubtedly, every company has a lot of new information for a new partner to absorb, but information is very different from "action steps." Action steps are specific things you can do to actualize a specific result that will lead to generating income. Example: Share your story, write up a social media post, host an event, or send a message. The good news is that these action steps are always simple and clear. The complicated part is encouraging yourself to do it.

Remember, success happens when you choose to immediately get out of your head and into your heart. That's when you will feel compelled to "just do it!" Why are you curious about your company and its opportunity? How do you see that blessing your family or other families? When you look at your household or among your closest friends and you picture their faces, how will you achieving your goals create positive change for them?

Can you go help one person by proving yourself right or wrong? Can you take action on one thing if it meant the start of a massive compound effect? Could you do one thing that is uncomfortable to prove to yourself you can do new things (and you won't die)? Can you go earn that extra $50 or $100, which may not seem like much, but is the proof that you *can* create extra income from home or anywhere? Can you do this for your children, your spouse, your loved ones or—heck!—for the love of yourself and all that you know you can be? Can you do this one thing differently? Will you silence your negative beliefs and start speaking possibility into your own life first?

Because, if you can't start here by speaking possibility into your life, then the truth is, you can't lead others. Leading others starts with first leading yourself. It means you lead yourself away from the negative voices, you acknowledge them, and then you lead yourself toward a new pattern of thinking. It means that when those familiar voices try to chime in next that you reply back with a new response. "I hear you, but I don't respect you, and furthermore, I no longer believe you are true."

Future leaders decide to literally reprogram their minds, actions, and lives. Here is where you make a conscious decision to experience a metamorphosis. You're going into the cocoon of your heart to take control over your mind. Like a wild horse you must tame, you hold the reins in your hand. Stop looking down in fear. Start looking up in courage. You can steer in any direction on any given moment that you *decide* to turn. You may be on a wild beast, but that beast is no wilder than you. You are way smarter, too, I might add. Crack the whip!

Sleepwalkers Awake

Are you aware of your self-limiting beliefs? Do you see areas of your life, skills, and capabilities in which you are lacking confidence? I hope so.

It may feel uncomfortable, but now I ask you to also step into leadership and choose joy. A person who is aware of areas in which he or she can grow, is a powerful human. This is someone who has the ability to transform. This is a person who has the ability to inspire others to transform. After leading yourself, the next step in leading others is choosing to let your example shine and inspire them. "Transformation" means to go through *a thorough or dramatic change in form or appearance*. If you want to inspire others to transform, then I must ask you, where is your dramatic change?

On December 11, 2012, my mother passed away. Something I had dreaded for so long had come to fruition, and it felt worse than I had imagined. When my oldest brother, Jason, had passed away from a car wreck in 2004, I only remembered completely collapsing. I crumbled from the inside out. As my heart shattered, so did every other good thing in my life. I ignored any other relationships in my life, I stopped going to my college courses, I started no-showing my job, and was fired as a result. I let my health crumble, and I lost all faith in anything good. I was twenty-two years old, and I wanted to give up on life because I couldn't understand how anything good could come from my thirty-six-year-old brother (who was a father to two young children) dying. So I coped by letting parts of me die, too.

That was an extremely difficult way to mourn. It took me losing a scholarship to see how quickly you can mess up potential in your life with even just a little bit of running and hiding. As I became aware of the wreckage around me that I intentionally created, I realized that this was no way to live and no way to honor my brother. It took me several years to correct that mess.

So when my mother—the woman I considered my rock—passed, I was distraught and of course, tempted to mourn the only way I knew how. But then, two little girls wiped tears from my eyes. I looked at them and knew that I couldn't run from them. I saw my husband who would never leave my side, and I couldn't run from him. I saw my life flash before my eyes the day my mother passed away. As my mother's life ended, I was just beginning mine.

I held her hand. The monitors beeped slowly in the background. Her breath grew fainter as the seconds passed. As I took in the events of my life, I was not proud. I was walking blindly, and when startled, I just ran in the opposite direction.

My mother's early passing left me with a blank slate. She inspired me to actually be brave for the first time in my adult life. I went home, and yes, I still cried my eyes out, but I was not angry. Because I decided it was no longer an option to walk blindly or to run away cowardly. I had no other choice but to take different actions.

I prayed for renewal that day. I prayed for God to come into our life like a flood to wash our lives clean, so that only good things could flourish, and so we could lead a new life.

All I can say, folks, is be careful what you pray for, for you just might get it.

Seven days later, we received another call from our mentor, and this time, it was an invite to our second event in Portland, Oregon. This event would only be three weeks after my mother's death. The old sleepy, cowardly Sam wouldn't have even entertained the thought. But just days after my prayer, I was already being given an opportunity. I was serious about my requests. I cried again, and I told Harold to book our tickets. That event was exactly what we needed, right when we needed it, and it gave us community, positivity, and the tools to grow even more.

From the moment we came out of sleepwalking, we stepped into the conscious choice to succeed or fail. Are you ready to wake up? Are you ready to truly take control of your life?

Sleepwalking seems easier sometimes because we are almost unaware of our failures. But trust me, it's not easier, and you will always know you're not content at some point of your life. It often shows up in numbing ourselves with the mundane, ritualistic things that temporarily fill a void: TV, food, work, cleaning, routine gatherings, and the kids' extracurricular activities.

We do a good job of keeping ourselves busy being busy, but it's just an illusion. I encourage you, if there is a void, let it be known. Get rid of the nonsense that is silencing the most important voices waiting to be heard—the voices telling you that you have unfulfilled potential to make the world around you a better place. Too much decision and not enough wisdom will land you in a world of trouble, so instead, lead with your heart and lean into doing the good work set in front of you.

Things to Ponder

1. Self-Talk: What lies do you keep repeating to yourself that need to go? Replace those lies with the truth: you are capable, you can learn, you can grow, and you can help others do the same.
2. Curiosity: "What if" is enough. Wake up every day

curious about growing in the right direction and you'll seek ways to grow!

3. Leader Without a Title: Name a few areas in your personal and business life where you can commit to leading yourself like the leader you deserve.

#SIDEHUSTLEHOPES

FIVE

Fight for Your Future

"A million miles away, your signal in the distance to whom it may
concern. I think I lost my way, getting good at starting over every time that
I return. Learning to walk again. I believe I've waited long enough.
Where do I begin?"
Walk ~ Foo Fighters

Knowing you need to let go and actually letting go are two
completely different things.

Often, we are preparing ourselves for the fact that we will
undoubtedly need to release our grasp and see whether we're
going to fall or fly. We hold on tightly with white-knuckled fists
to things that hurt us. Knowing if we let go, we might just get
some relief from that release. With every release there is a free-
fall first. It is a simple exchange for the cost of our freedom.

But who in their right mind wants to fall? That's why people rarely let go. That's why people rarely find their true freedom.

Little by little, Harold and I grew professionally and personally. It was absolutely amazing and so rewarding to see that, by choosing a different path, we were actually growing in all the ways we had hoped. Our side hustle was growing. We were actually earning a significant enough income that I was able to leave our brick-and-mortar business and work from home with our kids. I had achieved my big dream goal and knew I was on the right track. I was home caring for my babies and contributing to our income on our terms. It should be noted that we did all this with what little time we had left outside our full-time career.

We did not just leap blindly. We worked to bring in the exact income we needed for us to decide that it was feasible for me to only work from home.

Our marriage was on the mend—no, it was more than on the mend; my marriage was starting to thrive. I was truly happy, for the first time in such a long time. One hard push after another, we had given new life to so many wonderful things. A wonderful new location-free business, two healthy daughters, a great marriage, personal growth, and a brick-and-mortar business that was just fine. And though I was happy and on top of the world, our other business was the same roller coaster it had always been.

But I was still in denial. That business was my first baby. That business gave me a name in the community. It made me a somebody when I felt like a nobody. It also did many great things for Harold and me. That business brought a lot of wonderful people into our lives, it taught us the value of hard work; we learned to be entrepreneurs, and it broke the first seal about what we were capable of in relation to our family heritage. But we never really learned to work together in that business. It also brought a lot of toxic people who didn't share in our values or vision into our lives. It was a revolving door of problems—from employee issues, to lack of time and financial freedom.

Yet I held on. I held on because one day in 2006, I drew a pair of wings on a paper napkin and we created the would-be name of our future business. It's slogan, "To rise above," because in that business, I was dead-set to elevate myself and others to rise above their limitations. That business was supposed to be my savior, and a promise of a better future. It was supposed to do a lot of things, none of which were actually panning out.

I never pictured starting that business with my husband for it to merely be a temporary stepping stone. And so I held on tighter, because maybe there was something I wasn't doing right? Or maybe there's something my husband could do to make it finally work.

Well, he did. He actually turned around many of our systems, and the business was showing it could start earning us an income because it had stopped, dead-cold in its tracks. We put bills and employee payroll on our credit cards while anticipating potentially losing our home and that business, anyway.

Because we had a back-up income (thanks to our home-based business), Harold was able to take three months to focus on giving our primary business a heartbeat again. He spent so many hours away from home, missed dinner often, and never saw us in the morning. At the end of the day, all we had was a spent, stressed daddy. He saved that business, and he spared my heart yet again from the pain of having to choose.

Do we choose to see the writing on the wall? Do we choose to see that every day we anticipated the cry of urgency over our lives? Do we choose to see that we were slaves to that business—that it would never provide us hope but only hopelessness? Do I choose to let go of an unforgiving and incapable savior I fabricated on a napkin to leap into this new financial vehicle?

My answers then were often no, but not in my words. I answered yes in my words, and I was oblivious to the fact my actions did not support that choice. My pride in my creation would not submit. My fear of looking like a failure was stronger than my desire to explore a life without those problems.

That was until one day, when my persisting, faithful, and very tired husband came home after a long day of work absolutely speechless. He slowly walked about our kitchen until he reached a chair and sat down slowly. I looked at him in a way only a wife can, sensing the aroma in the air. Something was wrong. As Harold sat down, his head fell and collapsed into his hands as he began to cry, "I don't know how much longer I can do this."

He was exasperated, exhausted, and just completely done. Yet I knew that unless I did something different, he would never give up. He would continue to try to make things work at that business and break his back because he loves me. He cared about what I wanted and he knew I wanted that business.

Do I choose my pride or do I choose my husband? Do I

ignore the signs and wait for a day where he is smiling again to only anticipate the next breakdown at that business? Do I watch the degradation of my husband to the immense pressure of financial stress yet again, or do I decide that this ends right here and right now?

I sent everyone to bed early that night, and I stayed up. It was on that night that all my thoughts and decisions were finally going to reflect in my actions. I gave up my precious TV shows (I loved all things Bravo), I gave up my fear of failure, I gave up all my excuses. We were going to bring my husband home.

Honestly, it didn't feel like I was giving anything up. With that decision, I knew I was gaining more than my old world could ever provide. That business had to go. We—not just me —would rise above by letting go.

I literally cried over a basket of laundry that night as I vowed to move beyond myself and my own desires yet again. I was home loving the work-from-home-mommy life while my husband was suffering yet again at a job he didn't love. I totally and completely immersed myself into my faith, books (I wasn't a reader then), podcasts, trainings, events, and my relationships. If I watched TV, it was to watch a documentary for inspiration or education or to watch a movie with Harold as a stay-at-home date night. I said no to anything that would harm or compromise my *yes* to my whole family's future together.

Look, you're either all in or you're toe dipping. Toe dipping can create some good things, but you'll never create a masterpiece unless you dive right into the deep end. And I don't mean reluctantly walking into the deep end with your body clenched, head turned in the opposite direction in fear, nose pinched, and praying no one notices you.

Don't resist the leap. No, you must accept the leap and run wildly and excitedly toward the deep end. Just like a child would with limbs flailing about in preparation for the most epic cannonball; trying to make the biggest splash of your life. You need to feel the free-fall, and you need to make a splash!

When Plan "A" Plummets

What do you do when you've been diligent to make things right in your world, but all of a sudden, you see very clearly that your original plan is a flop? When you see that there is nothing you can do or should do to try to save that plan, and furthermore, continuing to do so is stealing the things you adore most in the world from you? You let go.

But the beauty is that we had a Plan B. Letting go of Plan A meant being able to admit that we didn't always have to be right about everything. There was hope beyond the scope of the plans we could create. You have the right to burn a few bridges when the time is right. That can be different for everyone.

Because we had put the effort and time into building something new while we worked on figuring out where the "old" fits in; when the time was right, we were actually able to let go of it. That is what we wanted to do.

When I was finally able to see our current reality very clearly, I saw the truth. I saw that no matter how much I poured into our original business, it would always present us with the same problems. No matter how much money it earned, or if we grew to multiple locations, the problems that business presented would never go away because they were part of that business' DNA. If we did, in fact, grow it, that meant we would scale those problems to a larger level, too.

Here's Your Wakeup Call!

We looked around and saw we were on the Titanic. That ship was going down quickly. And we realized we didn't have to go down with it because we had a perfectly good life raft we very intentionally placed in the right spot. We could wake up to the day when we could *all* leap onto that raft and sail away into the sunset. Have you ever stopped to ask yourself, "Am I aboard the Titanic right now?"

Do you know why people become stuck in situations they don't want to be in? It is because they only prepare for Plan A and don't stop to consider that the plan you do have may not be sufficient for the rest of your life. There is no Plan B or a dream job. We simply settle for a paycheck and a retirement plan and forget that we were blessed with special skills and talents.

Have you found a way to fuse your passion with your paycheck? There is a vehicle out there, but you have to open your eyes and search like your life depends on it, and you'll want to choose something that can evolve with you as you grow.

It is okay to look for better options to create the freedom *you* desire for *your* life. It is okay to look for a life raft that will sail you away to Tahiti. Who cares

how big and shiny the boat is—you are going to Tahiti!

Our first business was one-dimensional. There was only one way for us to help people, in one location, with one type of income, a certain employee type, and only one way to work that business. As our goals and desire grew from just being business owners to becoming #TheFreedomParents, so did our vision of what kind of life we wanted to live.

I went from being raised in poverty to finding the confidence to become a business owner. But then I had my first child, and it was no longer good enough for me to own a business that kept me away from her so much. That's when I decided I needed a work-from-home opportunity so I could do two things I love simultaneously: raise my children and work in my passion. Lastly, my marriage was alive and full of hope and love, but my love, my husband, wasn't with me, and he wasn't as happy as I was. As a result, we decided to grow our side hustle into our full-time passion project to create freedom for us as a family.

Is the plan you have set in place to create your desired freedom, multidimensional? Can it grow and shift as you grow and shift? Can it take you where you really, truly want to go?

Whatever it Takes

Do you have a glimpse of what freedom will look like for your family? Can you imagine living in freedom and chasing adventure instead of urgency? I promise you, it will be worth the work. Don't convince yourself you're crazy to think this might actually be possible for you. You are not crazy!

You'd be crazy to ignore the calling on your life. There was a prophecy bestowed on you to do great things; to be a role model for your children and their children to come. You are breaking the mold. You are giving value to things that people try to steal value from every day.

Together, we are drawing the line in the sand. We refuse to let the world push our families around any longer. Today is the day you stand on the front line and let everyone know that you and your family are made for more. And for what it's worth, as #freedomparents, we are not afraid to prove it to everyone watching and naysaying.

In fact, that's fun for us. We weren't always so resilient, but the more you learn to look at this as a fun game—the more you will become resilient to the external byproducts of change.

Say aloud with me: "Watch us grow and enjoy the show, because that's why we started this, anyway; we, the #Freedom-ParentTribe are dead-set on living our best life. This one life we are given is going to shine."

(And it's my party and I'll go to Tahiti in a tiny boat if I want to.)

"'Cause every night I lie in bed
The brightest colors fill my head
A million dreams are keeping me awake
I think of what the world could be
A vision of the one I see
A million dreams is all it's gonna take
A million dreams for the world we're gonna make"

A Million Dreams ~ The Greatest Showman

Things to Ponder

1. Let go or be dragged. Don't let your fear of failure be stronger than your desire to live your best life.
2. Rise above by letting go. If you had to be completely honest, are you gripping tight to something you need to let go of?
3. Defend your YES: When you say YES to building your family's future, what will you have to say no to in order to defend that choice?

#FightForYourFuture

SIX

Learning to Soar

"I know what you're thinkin', we were goin' down. I can feel the sinking',
but then I came around. And everyone I've loved before flashed before my
eyes. And nothing' mattered anymore, I looked into the sky."
Wheels ~ Foo Fighters

If I told you that we never felt anxious or overwhelmed, it
would be a flat-out lie. Darling, I have felt it, and I have felt it
big. And yet, I can't stand those two words. Those two words,
or things, are flat out liars and leeches. Anxiety, depression,
anger, and confusion have damned near try to steal any good
opportunity in my life. If you're anything like me, you probably feel the same.

Like a thief in the night, most of the time I never anticipated the wreckage coming. If there is one good victory that
was left in the place of anxiety; it's awareness.

Anxiety comes from the feeling or the desire to be at 100% completion without failures or flaws. Anxiety is anger + frustration + urgency = confusion; all tied up with a pretty little bow of convincing ourselves we are just overwhelmed. And what about feeling overwhelmed? Well, that manifests as we continue to ignore details in our lives piling up, going ignored, and just begging to be noticed. Yet we continue to walk right past the red flags.

Anxiety is the result of the pressure of the desire for perfection. But not just perfection. It's the desire for perfection *immediately*. It's the feeling of dreading the undone, while also somehow dreading getting the undone done.

It's a yucky feeling, and it's a prison. But this prison sentence is optional. No one likes it and yet everyone is subject to feeling anxious and overwhelmed. Here's the scary truth though; these two emotions depend on you giving them value. Anxiety and overwhelm cannot exist in your life if you do not put energy into the feeling.

If you don't put energy and thought into the feeling of anxiety and overwhelm, they have no option but to disappear. We then have no option but to pay attention and deal with what is actually nagging at us. You stop acting like you are the problem and start looking for solutions.

It sounds so simple, right? If it's that simple, then why are the majority of people struggling with beating this battle? (Yes, I'm saying you are not a problem and you are not an abnormality.) There's really no simple answer. But I can tell you that I was used to running from it instead of dealing with it. That is definitely *not* a good solution.

When this surge of feelings starts to collide with us, our basic instinct is to flee. But when you run, you lose the opportunity to learn and grow from the experience. Anxiety and overwhelm are almost always the result of procrastination and the lack of attention to certain details and signals in your life. Gone unnoticed and unaddressed, you will always struggle repeatedly with the same things in life. And you will always continue to tell yourself this lie: "I just can't." You will think you "just can't" take on anything more (even the greatest opportunity) because you cannot handle what you have.

Must there really always be another battle to fight? Yes, some big and some small. But with certain battles, you will gain so much freedom. Winning this battle will literally bring so much peace and perspective to your life. Winning this battle personally will equip you to come alongside the swarms of Americans that feel the same way every day. Every day, someone else is struggling to rise above the feeling that they must arrive at their final destination today with all pieces in place and nothing ever falling by the wayside. The sooner you realize you are not the only person who has ever dealt with anxiety the sooner you can get on with your life.

I'm right here with you. When you picture your final destination—whether it means becoming a million-dollar earner, helping a million lives, or simply replacing your current income with a job you actually love—the desire can be so strong and your current situation so undesirable that it's totally human to desire to be where you want to be right now. As much as we can desire that all day long, it's just not always realistic or possible. Your dream life will not be made in a day, because the greatest reward by far will be becoming the kind of person who *earned* that dream life. Snap your fingers and win the lottery, but you will bypass your true ticket to freedom.

Money will never be able to free a person who is a prisoner in their own mind.

"Do you not know that in a race all the runners run, but only one gets the prize? Run in such a way as to get the prize. Everyone who competes in the games goes into strict training. They do it to get a crown that will not last, but we do it to get a crown that will last forever. Therefore I do not run like someone running aimlessly; I do not fight like a boxer beating the air. No, I strike a blow to my body and make it my slave so that after I have preached to others, I myself will not be disqualified for the prize."
1 Corinthians 9:24-27

Do You Really Want Out?

Look, I used to be the queen of complicated. I would let my head take me down all kinds of rabbit holes until I was completely dizzy and unable to make any choices. That kind of life was a prison.

The complicated mind is often doomed to feeling anxious and overwhelmed. The complicated mind becomes paralyzed with indecision and lack of action. We feed this emotion by letting it take us for the worst ride of our lives, a never-ending loop. But you can stop this dead in its tracks. Right here, right now, I call B.S. on the "I just can't" attitude.

Dear Lord! Yes! Yes, you are going to notice your plate is a little fuller than usual. Can I ask you to STOP being scared of taking on MORE of the good things that will bring value to your life? Can I ask you to STOP saying, "I can't"?

Yes, your family and friends might give you slack because they are not used to having to share you or understand this new highly-aware and driven version of you. YES, if you commit to taking daily action and embracing structure, discipline, and the obstacle as the way to growth, you will end up inspiring customers and partners. Your calendar will not only be full with your family rock and your other rocks, but it will start filling up with pebbles and sand, too. Hear me; you can't grow if it doesn't get full; straight-up overflowing.

There will be times that you don't even recognize who you are because you've been so consistent that your business is actually starting to grow, for God's sake. Isn't this exactly what you wanted? You wanted new life and a new opportunity. So don't start trying to feed yourself lies again and submit to fear because it will wreck everything you've just created! No . . . You're not overwhelmed. You, my friend, have opportunities!

No . . . You're not anxious. You, my friend, are alive! Life is swirling all around you, and it might feel crazy, but *this* is what opportunity feels like; busy. Because, for the first time in a while, you decided to stop just using cruise control. You cranked that car up to one hundred miles per hour, and you are kicking up some major dust! This is what is supposed to happen.

If you are going to choose this path, don't forget to let go of things that keep you busy-being-busy and do not contribute to your future goals. You can protect your sanity, your calendar, and keep your family sacred. Heck, you can hire out laundry and housekeeping to protect your sanity and family, too.

I was pregnant with our third child when we were making

our big push for complete freedom. It was January—our anniversary month—and I so wanted that rank to be my husband's gift for two reasons; one, I promised I wouldn't get pregnant with our third until we had reached that milestone because it signified an income Harold felt comfortable would provide the life we wanted to give our children (and I accidentally got pregnant before that rank—oops!). Second, it also happened to be the income for us to start planning to bring him home and prepare to either sell or close our other business.

Guess what? We missed it that month. My heart ached; I was tired, five months pregnant, and crying over the kitchen counter—no, sobbing! I had failed. At that moment, I wondered if it was all going to be worth it. I was stressed, stretched, and desperately needing a break.

I lifted my head and reminded myself that I only doubted myself because I was still forced to live a double life. I was maintaining the lie of the career I no longer desired while, on the other side, I was trying even harder to build up our dream career. The resistance and pressure reached the greatest levels we had ever felt. I thought we might burst.

Did anxiety and overwhelm rear their ugly heads that night? Of course, they did. We prompted ourselves to a simple question, "Do we give up, or do we just kick the door down regardless and finish what we started?" Can you guess what we chose? We accepted the opportunity, door-kicking and all.

The next month, we hit that goal. It was Harold's birthday. I guarantee you; it felt just as good to have that gift as a birthday present. Can you guess what felt even better than that success? Not giving up. That night, we only cried for joy.

This is normal, and believe me, the dust will settle. We know this because we have been there before you. When it does settle, don't be surprised that your life will not be messier, but your life will actually be shinier.

Believe me, you have done harder things. I have had to pull my girls out of activities they loved because we could no longer afford it. I have had to bypass getting family pictures because of our income dropping from our previous career. Those things were hard with no hope of getting easier. But these hard times provided a promise of a better future.

We have kicked up so much dust with so much momentum that, for a short season, our life did get really messy! But we still had our "Big Rocks" in place, no matter what. So when we needed peace and perspective, we could get it.

Then that dust started to settle. We sold our business, and we were able to do so sooner than anticipated because all that momentum we created in our side-hustle turned into a full-on, legit money-maker. We put on our running shoes and started counting down to "Operation Bring Harold Home."

Little by little, our consistent action was rewarded by growth and the comforts of a new life. The growth was worth the push. Your growth will be worth the push, too, when you see the new life it birthed.

When life seems to be dunking your head underwater, trying to keep it there just another day, choose to anchor yourself to things that will create freedom. Make the decision that gasping for air is no longer acceptable. You can choose to be the lighthouse and not the sinking ship.

Structure, discipline, faith, and consistency all build a solid foundation that cannot be shaken. The storm might rise up, but it will never consume you. Those roots are strong and they provide good fruit, but what's even better is they will give you wings to soar.

It's these moments—the struggle and the striving—that really define us, shape us, and make us capable of leading others. It's rising above something as big as creating financial freedom that helps you easily glide over every day drama.

You start to see that everything that used to cause you anxiety or frustration was really just small and not worthy of your energy. You learn how to guard your heart, your mind, your family, and your future against things that could actually harm you. You become a warrior equipped with actual real-life weapons, tools, and skills to not just survive but to thrive! The little things will no longer faze you.

Oh my goodness, my friend, you will SOAR! You will soar because you learned to ground yourself first. Are you ready to release your shackles? Are you ready to see that you have wings to rise above it all?

"But those who hope in the LORD will renew their strength. They will soar on wings like eagles; they will run and not grow weary, they will walk and not be faint."
Isaiah 40:31

Things to Ponder

1. Anxiety = Alive. When you feel a bit anxious, take

time to sort through your thoughts. What is really bothering you? Then give yourself a break. Take a walk, or go to bed early. Sometimes, we need to process before we can progress.

2. Overwhelm = Opportunity: If there wasn't the ability to do more in front of us, then we could not be overwhelmed. Likewise, we would not have the opportunity to improve our situation either. Just be kind to yourself and prioritize a few key tasks daily instead of twenty.

3. Reminder: Do not allow your complexity to overshadow the simplicity of growing a thriving network marketing business.

#LEARNINGTOSOAR

SEVEN

Let's Talk Business

H ow does one grow to be a leader? They grow into a leadership mindset. I have always considered myself both an independent free-spirit, but also one who could follow someone's lead. But mostly, I really just wanted to do my own thing.

That's why I ended up dropping out of college to do personal training. It's also why I eventually opened my own business. I have always loved the feeling of having the freedom to be uniquely me. I found the idea of starting from nothing and growing to be something, extremely exhilarating. But, getting used to knowing that you can create your own path sometimes comes with some downfalls, too.

Working independently to create a business takes a good bit of self-discipline. Working independently to create a business alongside others, while encouraging them to create their own business, takes even more self-discipline. I had always thought I was extremely self-disciplined, but the reality was I was actually selfishly self-disciplined. I merely aimed to conquer the things that would bring me the instant gratification and comforts I desired. I worked for my world. You see, I could get by in my old world by simply letting others dictate my schedule. I owned my business, but other people were in control of my schedule. This created the illusion in my head that I was good at crafting my own schedule. I started a business, which created the illusion that I knew how to be my own boss. I had a family, which created the illusion that I somehow just inherited the super-mom gene. I had started a lot of good things, but I lacked the know-how to turn anything into a masterpiece.

Shenanigans and Self-Talk

To bring ourselves, our businesses, and others to the next level, we had to confront some convenient lies we were telling ourselves in order to find the truth. As you will see, our brains involuntarily operate in polar opposites unless we train them do otherwise. Why? We are conditioned to react.

Reactions are rarely thought through constructively. They are instant impulse decisions and thoughts that lead into behaviors that aren't suitable for growth. Somewhere in the middle of these extreme low or high thoughts, lies the truth. If you can apply your brain to this process, you will yield a wealth of knowledge, and you can apply this knowledge and pass it on to others. Have you ever had any of these thoughts?

- I know how to be my own boss / I need someone to be my boss.

- I am a hot mess / I've got it all figured out.
- I don't have time for this / I have all the time in the world.
- I have no self-discipline or willpower / I am extremely disciplined.
- I always mess things up / I never mess up.
- I am not structured / I am a structured person who needs more structure.
- I have to do this on my own / I need someone to help me more.

Egos and Excuses

Lies, lies, lies. I have worked both for others and for myself. One thing is certain; self-management is a skill that can be grown in many facets. I found working for people simple; too simple, to be honest. It wasn't challenging enough. Then there was the challenge of owning a traditional business, which definitely took self-management skills, but there were clear parameters to work. I had to work at certain times, on certain days, and do a certain type of marketing. It was pretty clean-cut, yet slightly more challenging, slightly more rewarding. Yet it was still limited in its scope of freedom.

Then there's operating a home-based business. The earning potential is vast, and depending on the company you're with, almost limitless. All you have to do is to learn how to structure the right amount of work time with the right amount of action steps. Oh, and you can work almost anytime and anywhere. The choice is yours!

It sounds great, and believe me, it really is; but to earn great flexibility takes learning to implement great structure. Isn't that odd? To gain freedom, we must be structured and disciplined.

Prior to bringing Harold home, I went from thinking I knew exactly how to be my own boss, thinking I had it all figured out and that I wouldn't need any help, because in twelve months (or less), we would be at the top of the company.

Then two years passed, and we were still at the bottom—ugh. Now don't freak out. It's not because we really tried. We didn't try very hard at all, and yet we were still disappointed.

How could we be disappointed with the lack of results we achieved when we compared it to the lack of work we did? Simple, because we went into our new business thinking we already had it all figured out. And we landed right on our tails for having that kind of ego.

One egotistical excuse after the next, we tried to justify further why we just couldn't seem to get this thing off the ground. We didn't have the time. We didn't have enough help —in general, from each other, or our coaches. We had to bathe the kids and put them to bed—which is a legit thing we need to do—but basically, everything was a reason we could not grow. Our heads felt like they were spinning while consumed with our current life. There was so much we could do to grow our new side hustle that we actually just did nothing.

And then something interesting happened; we finally attended our second event, and we saw something spectacular; people were succeeding. Yes, right there in front of our faces were people—lots of people—succeeding in reaching the top of the company and in less time than it took us to fail. Many of these people had far less time to invest, way bigger obstacles to overcome, smaller circles of influence, and honestly, fewer business skills than us, too. Yet, there they were succeeding nonetheless, and achieving the freedom we desperately desired.

But what impressed me the most by far was the type of people they seemed to become in the process; peaceful, powerful, competent, confident people who were making a difference in other people's lives and creating strong relationships as a result. That is what I wanted most—transcendence.

While we had squandered time and opportunity with our excuses and egos, others were making the most of their time by saying, "How can I?" instead of "I can't because . . ."

We returned home with a major shift in emotions and thoughts. Before we left, we were the hottest thing since sliced bread as "real business owners," but we returned home thinking, "What the heck is wrong with us? Why aren't we really doing this?"

I desperately wanted to play the victim and blame someone . . .

- Maybe if Harold would help me more at home or maybe if he would just let me quit our other business, we could succeed. Yep, it's Harold's fault; or . . .
- You know, my coach should really do a better job of telling me what to do. He doesn't call me enough. Yep, it's all his fault; or . . .

- Well, you know, my kids really just need all my attention. They don't like it that I'm working when they're home; or . . .
- I'm just a screw-up. I can't do anything right and I knew this would be the same. I just don't know how to do this; or . . .
- Maybe if I was more organized? I can't find any documents. This just isn't organized enough; or . . .
- I don't have time for this . . . I work all day, and the last thing I want to do is work more; or . . .
- My life is so crazy. I cannot imagine adding one more thing to my plate; or . . .
- My life is comfortable enough. I don't really want more.

Guys! These were all things I thought. And they were all excuses. Oddly, many of my excuses were also my reasons *why*. My *why* to build this location-free business that could earn a compounding residual income so that I wouldn't always be so tired, overworked, stressed, limited, broke, lacking confidence, and away from my family. I straight-up took my *why* and instead used it as my *why not*. Ugh . . . I didn't see that one coming.

Enjoying my husband and my girls (my son was not yet born) was the one way I wanted to spend my day every day, and yet all I could do was focus on the little bit of time I did have with them in the present versus thinking about how I could create more time with them in the future.

But that's the beauty of this business model. You can complain all day about why you can't be successful and then someone else not so different to you will show up and achieve all their goals. Why? Well, that person decided to drop the excuses and just embrace the obstacle as the way to growth.

That person didn't take no for an answer. I'm so glad two of my friends didn't say no.

Draw a Line in the Sand

About two years into our network marketing business, we received a Monday training call. New rank advancements were being celebrated for those who had reached the top ranks of the company.

I'll never forget the moment our friends—then strangers to us—broke down crying while sharing their story that night. She shared her aha moment, also known as their point of no return. For her, it was the moment she was in the hospital with her sick child. But it was not the fact that her son was sick. What broke her down, and eventually made her stronger, was when she needed to call her boss to ask for more days off to spend with her son in the hospital, and her boss told her no.

Can you believe that?! Someone else had power to tell another adult that she could not stay another day with her sick son! But this is the kind of stuff that happens when we are not in control of how we earn a living. You don't have to be okay with that. My friend, Susan, wasn't.

How did she reply to her boss? She politely stated, "I quit."

I woke up that night thanks to Susan having the courage not to just take no for an answer. I had more courage simply because I witnessed someone else being courageous enough to draw a line in the sand. Now, both of our families are living free.

The truth lies between the middle of freedom and structure. Yes, you need to create structure, and then you need to build the discipline to execute that structure consistently. Will you draw a line in the sand?

If you desire to move closer to who you want to be in the future, you have to draw a line in the sand, and you have to be brave enough to step over it.

You will have to be courageous enough to let that statement be obvious to those watching. Otherwise, you're just another silent bystander in the crowd watching others create the life they want to live.

The Need for Self-Discipline and Structure

That new discipline needs to be fueled by your *why*. Never forget the vision of your future. I used to be a pretty negative person. When I figured out I was abusing my *why* to use it against me instead of for us, I was able to make a sudden shift in my mindset. I started praying over my *why* every night when I went to bed and every morning when I woke up. I decided it was going to be the first thing I thought about when my feet hit the floor in the morning and the last thing I thought about when my head hit the pillow at night. I made it impossible for myself to forget just how important it was for us to build our #Freedomproject.

Here are a few other rules for success:

. . .

Know Your WHY

A monthly trip to TJ Maxx with $100 dollars in my hand was all I wanted, guys. Why? Come on, do you really need to ask? It's TJ Maxx! No, but seriously, there were a few people on my heart who needed what I had, and it just so happened that my husband and I often argued over my sporadic and spontaneous trips to TJ Maxx. I just wanted a little extra fulfillment of helping a few friends and a few extra dollars in my hand to call my own. A few extra dollars that didn't have to answer to anyone but the register at—you guessed it—TJ Maxx.

Deep in my heart, I wanted more, but for reasons I have already shared, I wasn't really aware or ready to start there. Shopping was my most immediate need. Wow, that sounds really lame, but it's the truth. Because earning even an extra $100 with one of those *things* would've blown my mind. And it did.

Secretly lurking around the corner of my mind, were bigger *whys*, but to be honest, I questioned just how hard I was willing to work to get there. I started with a really small shallow why—to go shopping. But as we leapt from one milestone to the next, a new why was unlocked.

Why did we want to succeed in reaching our goals? Because I had two little girls and an amazing husband I loved so much but rarely saw. We wanted a third baby, but deep down, we knew we would struggle to provide sufficiently for another child. We craved adventure—not just to travel, but to break out of the mundane daily mold we were living in. Harold and I could see that we were slowly dying on the inside while providing for the people we loved, but not in a way that we could be with the people we loved and the world we craved to see. I wanted to save my husband and my kids and other families from falling into this same pit. Now that's a *why* worth fighting for.

What's your why?

Be a Product of Your Product

If you can't be a walking, talking billboard for your company or for the one you're researching, then good luck inspiring anyone else to join you on this journey, too. This is the start of your story.

Network marketing is meant to be an industry of authentic transformations. That's why so many people don't last. If you're not completely committed to taking the leap and testing your product and offering on yourself, why would anyone else follow you? Discipline and structure are going to follow you everywhere you go in this business. If you've lacked integrity (as all of us have occasionally), running a home-based business is going to show you really quickly where you need to grow. And that's a great thing, because then you know where to put the work in to see results.

When we found our opportunity (a health company), we were already very fit. I was an avid half-marathon runner, loved lifting heavy weights, and lived and breathed all things health and fitness. We approached our company from the business side first; however, we knew that if I wanted to coach, I should experience the program. So I bought my business kit and client kit all on the same day. Some would have assumed I didn't have any weight to lose. They would assume wrong.

My results were amazing; I lost eight pounds I didn't realize I had to lose and saw my abs faster than anything I've ever tried before. I was hooked, and my results alone were the first push I needed to really get excited about sharing with other people, too.

Those eight pounds might have seemed insignificant to most other people. To people who desired to lose twenty, thirty and even over a hundred pounds, my story probably wouldn't even have a chance when sitting alongside theirs, right? Wrong. I was suffering in that dreaded Yo-Yo pattern for my entire adult life. I could get lean; I had pictures to prove it, but I could never stay there. I would always gain back the same five, ten, or fifteen pounds I had lost, and in just a matter of weeks or months, I was miserable yet again.

My prison didn't just contain me; it held many other victims with all kinds of weight-loss goals. I knew if I was suffering that there were many others who needed me to be their voice. I could not just leave them there. When you get out, you go back to get others out, too.

If you can get excited, you can open your mouth and spread hope with confidence. Find your platform. While almost everyone is embracing social media these days, some people are highly social and outgoing. You might do best getting off the ground with your business simply by sharing a short thirty-second story with your friends as they compliment you out and about. Or you might be like me and feel better building your confidence behind the screen of your phone or computer. Or you might be ready right now to just start big and do all those things I mentioned in addition to hosting events in some form.

You'll end up doing both, but it's totally okay to start where you feel strong. **Two basic skills every entrepreneur needs to become proficient and consistent in are *promoting and presenting* in various ways. It is the lifeline of your business.**

What if you're an introvert? Both Harold and I can understand how you might feel. The good news is you can train yourself to be an extroverted-introvert. The best way to do that is to just be truly excited about what your product and company has done for you.

Believe me, neither Harold nor I was looking for a new career that would basically turn us into public speakers. In fact, I used to joke that I would rather swim with sharks than stand up and speak in front of a crowd of people.

You may never need to do that. You might have leaders that love presenting, in which case you just need to learn to be an incredible promoter! But nonetheless, you will have to talk to people, and there might be actions that draw you out of your comfort zone. You will be nervous.

Look, I once blacked out just standing up to say my name in front of my college speech class. What was once one of my greatest fears is now one of my greatest joys! Now, to speak to a crowd of between three to six thousand people is quite normal.

Isn't that odd? I absolutely *love* getting up in front of a crowd, on a virtual call, or on a video and speaking life into people. To think that I once dreaded it! You get over it by doing it.

. . .

Connect with Your Mentorship and Trainings

There were definitely times we felt lost and didn't exactly know what the next step was for us to find our next client, to inspire our next coach, or to grow in our leadership. What I soon came to learn was there was always someone who knew how. Often, we could go straight to our mentors for that next step. However, one thing that grew us the most was just simply attending every possible training, whether it was on location, a call, or a virtual meeting. In the beginning, everything was over my head, and I didn't understand much of the content. BUT, I would always come away with one piece of wisdom or one simple action to implement. The key is that we implemented what we learned.

I learned the value of our mentors' time immediately. By far one of the best things our three immediate mentors ever did for us was encourage us with prophetic, motivating words. They (Alex, Craig, and the Millers) could have spent their time with anyone, but they always found time for us. I'll never forget the first time Harold and I got to spend a significant amount of time with David and Terri Miller.

These two were not only a wealth of knowledge, but they also were two of the most powerful leaders in our company and within our direct mentorship line. As the night was winding down, we were walking to meet up with other top leaders we admired and had never met. Harold and I were just barely scratching our way up the ranks and still had a way to go to see the top. We were honored to be among these people just as much as we felt unworthy. Then Terri introduces us to the crew. "Hey guys, meet Harold and Sam, our next presidential directors," she says casually. *Gulp!* Those were powerful, prophetic words! From that moment, I knew I did not want to prove her wrong, and we worked our tails off to make her statement a reality.

In addition, I would be able to hear from other leaders who were growing. I would follow them on social media and then figure out their rhythm. I learned to learn from those who were successful and had a proven track record. Then I duplicated those systems in my own style and used my own message.

At events, I asked lots and lots of questions, often to the other leaders who were training and presenting the most. These questions, looking back, were very novice questions— even silly (I'm quite sure I have embarrassed Harold a couple times), but they were questions for which I needed answers. Hence, my questions were important.

There were times my mentors were people who did not even know me, but I would look for opportunities to ask clarifying questions about whatever they had taught. It may have taken me longer sometimes, but eventually, I received the answers I needed to piece together a recipe for success that made sense in our heads.

I never waited to have it all figured out. I always found several things I could take action on immediately. Now these mentors are our friends because we rose to leadership following their examples. We go on trips with them and do dinner. A few of them even encouraged us to write this book. Life can be a beautiful full-circle experience.

I'd like to discourage you from asking people from other organizations to mentor you. This is called cross-lining in our company. Bring questions first to your direct line of mentorship. You might ask yourself first, "Am I watching all video trainings (live or recorded) available to me?" before asking questions you might be able to find the answer to yourself. If they cannot help you, then you might seek the opportunity to go further up, and at the proper time, bring questions to a line of leadership that is training the most for their company.

Please bear in mind; these people often have huge businesses of their own. Respect their time and respect their mentorship. These leaders have heard it all. The last thing you want to do is go to someone else with your complaints.

Be kind, grateful, and ask quick questions, being mindful that they have things to do and places to be. And do not be surprised if you are sent right back to your immediate business coach. After all, much of this is not rocket science, and perhaps, you might want to just trust your coach's lead. Remember, you are responsible for your own success. If you attend every event and training you are qualified for, then you should always have a clear path for success regardless of whether you have a leader of your own to personally teach you or guide you in strategies for growth.

Work Smart

I decided a long time ago that I was never going to be the color-coded, perfectly-time-blocked-calendar type of girl. I admire those who thrive from that type of organization, but for me, it's paralyzing. I've tried it, and all it does for me is make me over-analyze my schedule to infinity and beyond. I find myself putting every single little thing into my calendar.

"Baby sneezed at 6 a.m., check."

"Time to get the groceries, check."

Okay, I jest, but seriously, I panicked over getting my calendar just right. I had almost given up and bought into the lie that I was just a hot mess, and I couldn't really be my own boss. I was conflicted because we already knew what it was like to work ourselves to the bone.

We knew we could work harder than most, but we knew we had not learned to work smart. We were curious about this "working smart" and whether it was even possible. And then we found this jewe—a video by the late Stephen Covey, titled Big Rocks.

In this video, Stephen goes through a demonstration that was incredibly eye-opening for me. He placed a few big rocks in a jar, and each rock was labeled with main life priorities (family, job, faith, etc.). He then asked someone from the audience if it was full.

"Yes," she replied.

Then he pulled out pebbles and proceeded to fill the jar again.

"How about now? Is the jar full now?"

The woman smirked as if he had clearly stumped her, but still she replied, "Yes, I suppose now it is full."

But then he pours in sand, "How about now? Is it full?"

Of course, the reply was yet again a resounding "Yes." Little did this woman know that when she thought her life was just full to the rim, she still had plenty more gaps left to be filled.

The rocks, pebbles, and sand resemble our time and priorities. We have so much time to fit in so many things, but our problem is spending the right amount of time on the right things without neglecting the things we love most. From that day on, I decided that my family was the first thing to go into my calendar. I decided on the times that were my non-negotiable family time—the times I would not work. Turns out, it was a lot easier to block out the time I refused to work than to try to schedule my work first.

What are my BIG Rocks?

- Mornings with myself (peaceful time).
- Breakfast with my family.
- Dinner with my family.
- No work after 8:30 p.m. and Sunday off.

All those times are cell-phone-free, work-free spaces in my day, devoted to my *whys*. Any other time that was open I spent building our business. That's a lot of time, right? Believe me, you can find the time. It's better to do something with a little and build a future then to do nothing with a little and remain stuck in the present.

So when you sit down to your work hours, just ask yourself, "What does my business need right now?"

In our business, it's simple. We have four areas that we as entrepreneurs need to strive for growth daily, weekly, and monthly, and it's this:

1. Awakening new clients

2. Supporting clients
3. Awakening new partners
4. Supporting partners.

Rinse and repeat until desired goals are achieved. Now, there are some sub-categories in each area as to how we achieve that specific goal, but overall, it doesn't get more complicated than that.

If you have very few or no clients, then that's simple; you need clients. What do people in your company usually do to inspire new clients to join them? Do that.

Do you have plenty of clients and can easily bring on new clients monthly? Great, you're clearly mastering that beginner skill set, but are you building a team? If your answer is no or not consistently, then look at your client base. Who can you offer the opportunity to right now?

If you aim to do something every day to move your business forward, I guarantee you it will grow. So make sure you make this time sacred. Set some rules for yourself. Don't convince yourself you have to work 24 hours every day. That's a lie. Just take action. You need to commit some amount of time every day to the most important actions and don't be distracted.

Here are some examples of some of our favorite work times before we were full-time:

- Nap times.
- Early mornings.
- Car line.

- Driving (phone calls).
- Car rides (in the passenger seat there is so much you can do).
- Walks.
- During kid's TV time.
- Lunch time.
- Small thirty-minute window after dinner or immediately after putting kids to bed.
- While one of us bathed the kids, the other would work.
- Alternating story time at bedtime, the other would work.
- Visits with grandparents.

Not a long list, but that's the beauty of this business. It's simple if you choose to make it so. There are a few specific areas of building a successful direct sales business that demands your full attention and maybe even require that you should sit still. Figure out which of those tasks need to be their own "big rock" in your business and dedicate a weekly time to "clock in" as your own boss.

Many other things can be done on-the-go or while you live your normal life. For example, social media posts can be done as you go about your day. Feel free to follow me on Facebook and Instagram @TheFreedomParents. I share the things I'm learning, overcoming, or just simply enjoying in our daily life. I can reply to a text or a do a quick phone call while I cook dinner. The difficult part of choosing a simple business to grow is that we humans are complicated and often like to make simple things complicated with our over-thinking and our emotions.

Now, I'm going to tell it to you like this; I have told you how to do it, but the truth is very few of you will. You will overcomplicate it or underestimate it. But if you prioritize what I have told you, you will absolutely grow your business and a skill that you can pass on to others. The one or two of you who do will thank me a year from now for the freedom you've created. Do not pull your complexity into the simplicity of growing a thriving home-based business.

Your List

This is a simple task every company utilizes from the very start of every new partnership. The names on your list will make up the future lives you impact with your opportunity because we, as people, will steer where we stare, having no idea of who you would like to help when you are starting your business. This will cause you to walk around aimlessly in the dark.

You have chosen a handcrafted business, and that means you, my friend, get to build a business of your own design. Sure, we love all people and will help many different types of people from all different walks of life, but the fact remains that you already know people in your life that you would love to be talking to regularly, helping achieve their life goals, and traveling with to events. There are people in your life with whom you already know you will just hit it off immediately.

Often, people will start off with their family and friends. I get it; that's a comfortable place to start. Your family and friends will always love you, right? Should your loved ones think you're crazy for doing 'one of those things' they'll just forget by the next family holiday and move on. After all, they have seen you at your worst, anyway. This won't be the first time your family has to talk you off the ledge.

That said, family may be easy to approach, but let me be the first to tell you they can be the most complicated. It's just how family works. They want to protect us even from things they don't understand.

We didn't want to be talked off of this ledge. We were ready to leap! It was for this very reason that we didn't do just what our family and friends expected; we didn't go to them first with our opportunity.

Now, we did educate them and we did pull them into our circle so they knew what we were doing and why, but we did not try to convince them to be our first clients. We built our first list with people who respected us outside of the family circle. We looked at our current business, we looked at the places we went to weekly, and we looked at other areas of life in which we were connected with people, even social media.

We sat down and created a list of one hundred names. While there was family on that list, it was because we did have hopes of helping them in the future as we helped others; their trust would grow because we grew credibility.

You may be thinking now, "One hundred names? I can't come up with one hundred names!"

Yes, you can. I thought the same thing, but when I got tired of my business not growing, Harold and I finally sat down and decided we were not getting off of our sofa until that list was complete. We pulled out our address books, contacts on our phone, friends on social media, our wedding list, and year books. We wrote down the names of people who made our coffee (including "Nice guy at Starbucks with beard," because sometimes we did not even know these people's names yet).

We thought about the qualities of certain people we liked to be around, including: kind, successful, authentic, structured, relational, big heart, busy, and loves God and their family with their whole heart and life.

Our list became this beautiful centerpiece in our business that steered our focus of who was going to be not just our future dream team, but rather who were the people we actually do life with. Your list is a reminder of intentionality. It is how you intentionally build relationships and become curious about other people.

It is not something to be manipulated or abused. *It is definitely not a list of people to cold-call and bombard.* It is a tool to show you where you want to learn to build relationships with people with whom you will get along and can work as a team. Because, the truth is, not everyone clicks in this life. It's good to help people who challenge you and that aren't your cup of tea; they are often some of the most rewarding ones to see succeed as they grow your character and understanding immensely. But the other eighty percent of the people you serve should be the ones you hand-selected and can enjoy living life alongside.

Rejection

Worried about what people will think? Well, they will think

it whether you hear it or not. Why are we so terrified of being told "NO"? It doesn't make sense, but most of us shudder at the thought of hearing that two-letter word—I know I did. Do you want to know how I got over it? Sure, you do!

Well, I simply decided I needed to hear "NO" more, and furthermore, learn not to give up when I heard it.

You see, when someone tells me "No" now, all I hear is, "Not right now," or "I don't know yet." People don't understand that which they have not lived or seen. They are going to tell you no and this does not mean that is where the journey ends. I have been told no so many times by people who weren't ready to become healthy or who just couldn't see themselves as a partner in our business. The biggest mistake we can make here is to just accept that as a final answer and move on. Talk about making that person feel as though you couldn't get what you wanted from them and so they became obsolete in your life.

Instead, I continue supporting these people, being interested in their lives and—if their circumstances change— offering the opportunity again. I just assume that I do not know what is actually best for that individual, and as this person grows and gains clarity, he or she will still have the opportunity to say yes when they feel the same way I do and see what I see in them. "No" is not an insult, it is just a pause button.

Following Up

The gold is in the follow-up. We have all heard this said. It is totally true. But how we do the follow-up is even more important than just following up. One, have a list for your follow-ups. Two, you can do a direct follow-up once or twice before you need to back off. A direct follow-up is specifically asking if your potential customer is ready or if they have more questions. After you have done this, you want to make a shift immediately. I don't follow up to get a sale. I follow up because I care about the person I'm reaching out to and because I believe in them. I consider this a window to prove to them that I am a person of integrity and that they are more to me than just a number. As Harold always says, "We contend for their WHY until they are willing to do so themselves . . ." I also assume that they are not ready just yet and this window of time will help them be truly ready to work with me in the near future and knock it out the park.

This is a phase to develop relationships and establish trust. And it's simpler than you think. If you see these people in person, you can have a casual conversation. If this is online, you should also just have casual conversation. Comment on her cute outfit, notice how adorable his family is and ask questions . . . "Hey, how is your holiday going?" or "Wow, I can't believe how big your son is getting! Are you finally sleeping through the night?" Following up is about staying present and not constantly trying to sell people. The best salesman in the world is not one that is constantly trying to close the sale but rather the one who is constantly building relationships and trust.

If You're Not Having Fun . . .

Can I be the realist here? Life is not all fun all the time. I cannot stand when people say, "If you're not having fun then you're doing it wrong." Ugh, shoot me now. No, this will not be fun all the time and hear me loud and clear, that does NOT mean you are doing it wrong. Becoming a successful entrepreneur is WORK. And look, I love my work, and it is very fun now, but while we were growing, we felt the pains of that growth. There is nothing wrong with you for feeling the pain of growth and not feeling like it's all fun, confetti, and balloons.

When you commit yourself to learning new skills and putting new skills to action; you may feel stretched. On the other hand, you absolutely can look for fun and be a fun-maker every day. The things that will stretch you now won't in time. Whatever actions you decide to take on will make you stronger. Whatever actions you decide not to do will not grow you. It is very simple. In the beginning of any growth comes pain—or the stretch, as I like to call it. As you stretch, what may feel like discomfort now will actually not phase you in the future. Yes, that means your initial discomfort will become comfort, and what was not fun in the beginning will become fun with your growing competence and confidence.

As you aim to stretch and grow, the fun also lies in these victories! Take note of your growth even when you think no one else can possibly notice. Don't be so tense! Commit to being a fun-maker in your life every day, especially on stretch days. That's true peace. Do you want to know what is always fun? Turning on some music and shaking what your mama gave you.

· · ·

Things to Ponder

1. Stretch: Are you guilty of sometimes making your "Why" your "Why not"?
2. Big Rocks: Prioritize the actions that have been proven to grow a business. Do them daily.
3. Focus: When you implement structure, how will it free you personally?
4. Implement: When are your next opportunities to attend a company training whether it is a conference call, video meeting, recorded training, or live event? Do you have it set in your calendar with an alert!?

#FREEDOMPARENT

EIGHT

Counting Stars

"Lately I've been losing sleep. Dreaming about the things that we could be. But baby I've been praying hard, said no more counting dollars, we'll be counting stars."
Counting Stars ~ One Republic

How did we go full time? There are some logistical things I will leave you with before we close this chapter, but none of those are as important as these very first steps:

1. Learn to Count Stars.
2. Put the focus on yourself and then quickly take the focus off of yourself.

We went from thinking we were all-that-and-a-bag-of-chips small-business owners, to barely keeping our heads above the water. When we poured into our marriage and made that shine, our finances then crumbled. As we built our direct sales business and inched closer and closer to bringing Harold home, our extended family was in complete turmoil. Believe me, once again, we had every reason to only focus on ourselves and our lives, and no one would have faulted us. In fact, everyone would have thought we were completely normal for just giving up and walking away, and you know what, they would have forgiven us.

We would have earned a complete pass for turning inward to our problems, giving up on our goals and tuning out the rest of the world. But here's the thing, we would not be able to forgive ourselves for giving up.

There was one thing that helped this person, me, who typically ran (like hell) in the opposite direction of the opposition. For the first time in our lives, we had something that was bigger than us to fight for, and we could see so clearly that there were people depending on us; people we already knew, people who lived in our home and some we did not even know yet.

It could've been so easy and obvious for us to feed into the very real urgency of our current situation. That urgency to mend our finances, to check off our business-building action list could have been more than apparent to the people on the outside who were watching us and waiting to see if we were going to fail and flop, or if we were the real deal.

Let me tell you a secret: to become the real deal in direct sales, you have to really become the real deal. There are some that fake it, but ultimately, it always shows up later. You can't build an empire on sand. That means that, no matter what is going on in your life, you are consistently choosing the high road and constantly looking for ways in which you can serve others in creating good despite the chaos in your life. It means you actually commit to doing the work!

At least, that's what it means to me. Yes, we could have given up, and years later, no one would have remembered, but this became about more than merely our failure. If we chose to give up, then we would have stolen the opportunity for others to succeed. If we gave up, we lost integrity, and we lost the chance to give others a chance to break free.

"Direct Sales is an honorable profession, but unfortunately, many people have just done it in a dishonorable way without even knowing they were doing so." ~ Harold Lee Prestenbach, #FreedomDad

Our industry has received a bad rap. The need is obvious, but many people are oblivious to the right path to their desired outcome.

You need a team, and right there is where the mess starts for so many people. They need a team—a big team—to achieve their dreams, and so the scavenger hunt begins. We've all experienced it. Well-meaning people focused on a dream of their future pinging us out of the blue with their, "Hey! Want to try my product and opportunity?"—all over social media posts and messages.

But you forget one thing—or fail to see it. Your future team doesn't need more of you being scripted and "salesy." Your future team needs more of the real you. I applaud those of you who may have made this mistake because you simply took imperfect action. However, no one feels special about getting scripted messages we know every single person in your friend list received as well. There is a point at which, if we hope to succeed, that we have to commit to take progressed action instead of blindly shooting arrows into the dark. We must hone our skills.

Your future team needs a leader that has goals of their own, but who can be more focused on helping others reach their goals at present? A great network marketing leader becomes genuinely excited for the people he or she inspires and leading them into the action that drives their daily focus. A leader is hopeful for others in the face of adversity whether that adversity is in his or her own life or that of their team. A future leader learns the correct way to build a business and then teaches their team through first-hand experience.

If you haven't caught on yet, "stars" represented for us the people in our lives who desperately needed us to succeed. These were the people who desperately needed us to believe in them and in the fact that our goals and their goals were aligned. Instead of counting hours, setbacks, limitations, the workload ahead, naysayers, or fears; we learned to count victories and the people who dared to dream so big that they also dared to take action. We quickly learned that if we could find one star and encourage them to see the potential in themselves, then we could find more stars that desired to shine, too. Now, that is way more fulfilling and fun than the way I started out.

From Zero to Hero

See, I found myself in the same position as many new and excited network marketers. I would offer the opportunity, someone would say yes because I was clever, confident, and excited enough to convince them (I didn't even realize I was doing this), and I would count my victory because I caught that fish. And then something funny happened, which was basically nothing. Nothing happened!

My first few partners never signed anyone. They never helped even one person! There are few things as frustrating as trying to build your dream team and being unable to bring on any partners. Yet, bringing on partners who do nothing would definitely take the cake.

I was good at "getting" people, yet awful at inspiring people for "all the right reasons"—their reasons—to actually make a difference in someone else's life.

The excitement about the opportunity and what I was creating for my life overtook my emotions so much that I forgot the person on the other side of the phone was someone who had goals of his or her own. I was crumbling under the pressure of being awakened to my desires for my family's future, and it was showing.

Clearly, they had said yes after all to an opportunity, but WHY were they were saying yes? I was clueless. Because I lacked the awareness and attention to such important details, I took what may have been a perfectly capable and inspired person and reduced them down to a zero. I stole their ability to develop their own compass for their future.

And so there my first partners were, reduced to nothing but a pretty name in the back office site of my business with nothing but zeros following their statistics. They had no future because I didn't ask them what they wished that future to be. I had never learned their goals, their hopes, or if they had even one person they wanted to help. I was in a rush to get to the finish line and I was just taking names.

As soon as I realized that I was coming at people from the wrong angle, I desired to change it immediately. Yet again, for a moment, that familiar feeling set in; "I don't know how to do this." Instead of keeping this in my head, I decided to speak it aloud to Harold who, at the time, had invested more time in his personal development and leadership skills than I . . . His response was simple, "Help people obtain what they want, and in turn, we will naturally achieve our goals, too."

I thought about this for a moment and realized again the steps were simpler than I had made them. If I helped people reach their health goals (the result of our program when done well), then focused on the people who wanted to share their results, and helped those people inspire other people, then we would indeed build a business. But even better, we would build a business built on integrity, results, and the long game. If we could teach people to reach their goals and celebrate people for reaching their goals, then we would build something greater than a large team; we would build a family—a family of people united not in blood, but in hope, perseverance, and character.

It seemed like a lofty task—even a great deal of work—but something told me that I had already spent a great deal of time breaking my back on things that would leave me broken forever. I knew that how I was spending my hours was already tiring and taking the best years of my life away from my family. I knew that we were destined to work, anyway. If that's the case, then this is my season to be tired and work hard—well, darn it! We might as well make this really epic. We might as well work hard for a worthy reward in the future.

Becoming a Tribe

That was indeed the moment it clicked for me as a business coach. I had a new song in my heart. No, really, I had a literal song in my heart and in my head. The next morning, I woke up with the song "Counting Stars" on my mind. It was like a weight had been lifted off my chest. For the first time in this business, I realized it wasn't all about me!

The lyrics pressed into my heart. It was not only something I could tap my feet to, but it was a rhythm I could dance to in our business that so happened to remind me of a scripture. One that reminds me of God's promise for abundance.

He took him outside and said, "Look up at the sky and count the stars—if indeed you can count them." Then He said to him, "So shall your offspring be." Genesis 15:5

Could it be true? Would our legacy and our dreams be the start of an incredible domino effect that would simultaneously release and free others to achieve their dreams? I had no other option but to believe in that unknown future. Not knowing what lay ahead was actually captivating.

There is a promise for your life. I knew that our future promise was one of freedom. Freedom for us, our children, and many families to come.

I trusted that promise, and I trusted that it started with just a few of the right people. The more closely we listened and the more simply we obeyed, the more we continued to receive confirmations that we were on the right path. When our third child, our son, was born on 5/15/15 at 7:15 a.m., you'd better believe it was no coincidence. Just like his name, Stellan, which means "star" is no coincidence, either.

If that's not convincing enough for you that there are messages sent out into the world for all of us, we'll end with this juicy little detail here. When we sold our previous business, it was exactly one year after our son's birth. We celebrated his first birthday on a Sunday and the next day, Monday 5/16/16, we were in the bank signing over our business to the new owners who were sent to us through word of mouth.

Isn't That Curious?

Why does it matter? Why would you want to put in that time and effort to connect to so many people? Should it be this hard? Only you can really answer that for yourself, but I can tell you why it mattered so much to us.

Well, for one, a lack of money brings a lot of tension. When you're already feeling the pressure under your financial woes, striving for more money can, well, only create more pressure. It's a crazy paradox. The very thing you really do need more of, is only going to stress you out either while obtaining it or losing it, but financial freedom will seem like such a far stretch. That's why most people just walk away—they don't like that new tension. We are comfortable with our normal levels of tension, and though it may never release, we are accustomed to that pain and can just learn to live with it, right?

Nope. It will always nag you. If you have to earn money, it

might as well be earned in an epic way. You might as well be forced to grow in the process. The song, Counting Stars, actually says, ". . . no more counting money, we'll be counting stars!"

I, too, disliked the discussions about money when it seemed to have such a negative connotation in our life and it was causing us so much pain. But I loved the discussions about how many people we were helping, and I loved seeing that grow. We loved seeing the direct impact of helping people reach their goals in correlation to us hitting ours, too. For a season, I didn't want to think about money if I didn't have to. I just wanted to help people.

When I met one of our partners, she was a stay-at-home mom who was homeschooling her seven children—yes, seven children. When she started her business, it was as a means to continue doing what she loved and helping her family pay off their credit-card debt. She didn't have to tell me, even though I'm honored to be trusted with details far greater than this.

I knew just how hard their life was. I knew that money was scarce. I knew because, remember, I am one of seven children myself. So a few years into developing her business, she called me, and all I heard was tears of joy. My joy could not be contained either as I pictured my mother in this woman and what this kind of freedom would have meant to my parents. This woman single-handedly worked from home as a homeschooling mom of seven and paid off their credit-card debt while bringing in a significant yearly income. Now that's what I mean by focusing on people you can help. These are the kinds of people who want to help themselves just as much as you want to help them.

Secondly, as you have come to see, we are no strangers to pain or loss and—you know what they say about people who assume—but I'm going to go there anyway . . . I assume you're no stranger to pain and loss either. But my friends, despite the new cycle of crazy going on in our lives, we were at peace for the first time. We were happy even while crying for others; we were fulfilled, and we were busting at the seams with purpose even though our finances weren't exactly where we wanted them. It felt good—no, it felt amazing!

But not that long ago, we were on the verge of divorce, losing a business, and crumbling under financial pressure. Our life had turned around. Then I remembered the old "us" and saw the same situations, only with different sad faces. I saw the moms and dads out there who were still stuck in that prison, screaming on the inside for someone to help them. My husband was home for dinner now, but what about the dads out there who couldn't be home for breakfast or dinner?

I pictured my dad and his multiple panic attacks. Nobody ever threw a rope for him to get his head above the water. I pictured my mother—the woman who birthed seven children—and her many bouts of depression, barely able to cope with the immense responsibilities of caring for her large family while having no help and no reprieve.

I remembered Harold telling me stories of his house burning down as a child and the unpredictable situations forcing his family into financial stress and how his dad delivered pizza after working twelve-hour shifts. I looked at Harold's mother, our angel, who supported us through it all. Through our hard times, she was there, often not taking a paycheck. She watched our children so we could pay our bills, knowing that she, too, was having difficulty paying her own bills at the same time. I knew she understood. I knew my mother-in-law had been where we were, and probably even worse.

I saw my generation so clearly, and that despite the advancement in technology today and an increase in college education, we were no different to our parents. We were trapped in a cycle we never asked to repeat—a cycle they themselves never asked for, either.

While we thought we were stepping up to live the American dream, we realized—after we dragged our tired bodies through the door after a long day of work—that there's nothing left of us to give. So we sit on the couch, turn on the TV, and kiss the little faces around us while trying to convince them (and ourselves) that we are paying attention until everyone scurries off to bed. Ah, the bed! The last place we have to retreat from this never-ending cycle until the alarm goes off again.

I knew we were not the only people trapped in that cycle. Furthermore, I knew we were not the only ones seeking to break free. One by one, as our team grew slowly at first, we were regularly reminded that we were right. We were not the only ones suffering, and we certainly were not the only ones who had dreams and goals of creating freedom in a variety of ways. As we became curious about what others desired to create in their lives—whether it was health, disposable income, to serve mankind, or to replace incomes—we felt something we had never felt before: simplicity.

All of a sudden, our eyes were open, and we knew exactly what kind of people we were looking for: people like us. People with whom we shared a common chord. People who were motivated by similar things in life.

There is nothing more rewarding than helping others achieve their goals—nothing. We have hit a lot of personal goals and they're very rewarding. However, elevating people into their dreams comes with the pure bliss of liberation for many.

"When one man, for whatever reason, has the opportunity to lead an extraordinary life, he has no right to keep it to himself."
~ *Jacques Cousteau*

Once You Give, You Must Receive . . .

As our team continued to grow, I found that it was about so much more than us serving them. My pregnancy was coming to an end; I had a few months left.

Harold and I were so tired and yet so excited about life! We were about to have our third baby. We hit that huge milestone in our business and every month after that, our business goals continued to compound. We loved the people with whom we were doing life. We were on the rise to a new life, but here is where we all will continue to go through training.

Our on-top-of-the-world rise would be interrupted. Just days after walking into leadership within our direct sales company, I received a call that my sister, Shenandoah, had passed away in her sleep, leaving behind her two young boys. Six months later, my sister Elisha passed away, too.

Yes, we were finally winning our battle, and at the same time, two of my sisters lost their battles.

Getting that call rocked my world. I guess somehow, after my brother died in a car wreck, and we lost my mom, Harold's grandfather, and Uncle Andy—all in 2011, I somehow thought there was a cap to all the pain one could experience in this life.

I don't know about you, but sleeping on the floor of a hospice house with your three-month-old son will really do a number on a heart you're trying to allow to beat stronger. As I held a pillow over my face to silence the sobbing coming from my mouth, I heard my sister sobbing in the next room, wondering why—on what may be her last day on Earth—she could not see her five-year-old son and seven-year-old daughter to say "I love you," one last time.

I spent several days at that hospice house trying to comprehend the incomprehensible. I had been in and out of hospitals with my sister for months prior. We all knew why this was happening. Despite being there as the doctors explained to her that she would never be a candidate for a liver transplant because she was an alcoholic, none of this made sense still. Truth be told, we had been in and out of rehab centers with my sister, Shenandoah, since her teen years. Honestly, I had always thought they would eventually win their battle. The shock of it all was excruciating. I never got to say goodbye to Jason and Shenandoah. One day, they were just gone. I did get to say goodbye to my mother and Elisha. Neither situation feels good. You can't make sense of such terrible things like this except for yourself. How we decided to process the difficult times mentally and spiritually will decide how it shapes our future selves.

I lost two sisters to the prolonged effects of substance abuse six months apart, each shortly before their birthdays. One would have turned thirty-seven and the other would have turned thirty-six. Not one, but two sisters died on the inside first because of the long-term effects of chronic anxiety, depression, poverty, and lack of purpose and fulfillment.

I am thirty-six now as I write this book, and it's hard to imagine my life stopping now. My sisters each had two young children who needed them. Our typical thoughts would be, "How could they be so selfish?" But I tell you, I wish they actually would have been *more* selfish.

As they experienced the struggles so many people do—seeking love, trying to provide, being unable to pay bills, and divorce—at what point does a person finally break? How will he or she break? Will they just decide to let parts of them die internally and become numb, or will they seek external sources to mend the wounds? Until we understand the depths of our void and then aim to fill it, we cannot heal. And you will fill that void somehow—whether it's socially acceptable and done by the masses, or if we turn to something stronger because the pain is too great. Children can do a lot for a broken heart, but not even children can mend a person who is continuously beaten down by life. If we have emptiness in other areas, it will consume us.

Maybe that was when I should have quit? The resistance was so strong and my heart was so broken. Why push? Why pick up the phone? Why make a post on social media today? Because people depended on me. Others were out there currently being beaten down by life, and for them, there was still a chance. I didn't give up because my sisters depended on me to do something different with my life so that women and men just like them would have the chance to live.

To so many it may have seemed wrong, but to me, it actually felt right. In a time when I was so overcome with sadness, I actually had something that also brought a smile to my face. Supporting my clients and our partners allowed me to find goodness in a situation in which I struggled to see any goodness. Sharing our story allowed others to come in and support us during those difficult times; something I hadn't experienced when my mother and brother passed.

In my family, we rarely saw the beast of addiction beaten. However, through the madness of death came people who had beaten addiction and could share their story with me to provide me comfort and understanding in a time when explanations were nowhere to be seen. My prayer at this time was simply that God would show me that this beast could be beaten. I asked him to show me victorious people on the other side of such a consuming disease. To my surprise, right when I needed it most, these people fell into my life. Some of the people were either clients of our program or coaches on our team who were brave enough to share their story of victory with me (and many others) because I was brave enough to share our story of defeat.

I never knew just how important it would be for others that I was learning to honor our struggles so openly. But on a moonlit stroll after dinner at the Sundance Resort in Utah, one of our newest and fastest-growing partners melted my heart when she suddenly just came out and said, "Thank you for giving me my purpose back." She was a recovering alcoholic who had spent the past two years getting her health back in order. She shared with me that she was never really sure her brain would work the same after overcoming such an ordeal.

My friend and partner was a talented and bright woman who lost a bit of herself in her addiction. Her fear was that she would always bear a weight that she would never quite recover from, but in our world, she had discovered a new voice and a new strength. In this world, she could be honest about who she was and what she was overcoming, and she could use it to help others, too.

The people we poured our hearts into shared their dreams with us; they came to our side. They showed up at funerals, sent flowers, cards, and food. For the first time in a long time, I didn't feel alone. For the first time during such a difficult time, I didn't have to worry about going in to work or not. I was where I needed to be, when I wanted to be, holding my sisters' hands or hugging her sad babies, and no one cared whether I was clocking in.

I never pictured our direct sales business creating quite this amount of freedom for us—who would? I never pictured creating so much discernment and a structure that supported growth and healing. But in that season, it was the exact freedom I needed. I needed friendships, purpose, and a clearly lit path to keep me on my feet. Turns out we actually ended up needing the team I thought needed us so badly, but not to just hit some rank. For a family that was once unraveling, our team unknowingly knit us back together again, thread by thread, by allowing us to serve them. We had to learn to accept their friendship at some of the best times and hardest times in our life.

Be a Magnet

You don't always have to look perfect. Newsflash: You are working with real people who have real emotions and are going through real life. Proving you are progressing is the best evidence that you have what it takes to help others succeed. People desire progress, not perfection. Likewise, people desire to be in business with people who actually care about them.

During that time, I was a mess. I cried a lot, and that's the understatement of the year. Y'all, I had my life together in other ways. I kept my focus clear and my tasks simple. I made my goals, my team's goals, and the future of my family a priority, no matter what. It was cathartic. Instead of falling into a deep depression that could further tear apart our future and the future of others, I leaned into the pain.

If you're going to be the success you want to be, then you are going to need to elevate people into the success they want to be. Although you're not required to come into the game with your swagger wagon all perfectly polished, you do have to get your act and your life together in the presence of pain, rejection, and forks in the road. People don't quit their goals because life got easy. People quit their goals when life gets hard. Learn not to quit when life gets hard, and you will learn how to succeed.

You are a magnet. The parts of yourself that you shine will show, and actions speak louder than words. How you live your life will be the very thing that attracts people to you, or repels them from you. Your future team—people who have not even reached out to you yet—will watch how you handle yourself in your daily life and use you as the rule to which they measure their desire to grow into the business, too. That does not mean that you have to be able to serve up the meaning of life on a platter. You just get to wake up each day and ask yourself, "How will I rise above today?"

Most of your team will not come into the game wanting to know how to become a millionaire in a year (I would be very cautious if they did!). Your team is not looking for you to get the "Parent of the Year" award, and they certainly aren't looking to see if you're driving the most expensive car, or whether your house is always clean. It would be nauseating for anyone to see what appears to be the image of perfection and think that they, too, need to become that to be successful. Because deep down, we all know that we fall very short of perfection.

I don't know about you, but I want to see a leader who can be both polished and ready to go, but then also rock the "messy bun getting it done" T-shirt that might have two-day-old spit-up on it, too. That tells me that I'm following someone who may not always have all the answers, but is okay with figuring it out as they go. That tells me they're okay with handling the temporary mess to find the lasting message. That tells me they possess something most don't: resilience. That tells me that I can do it, too.

Resilience shows that there are people who bounce back. Given the opportunity, you will hopefully grow into the kind of person who doesn't just fall flat on your face every time you have a hard day, but rather become the kind of person who falls and never stays down long. You bounce back.

Your team is looking for grace under fire. They want to see that you are just as real as them. They want to know that your laundry and dishes occasionally pile up. They need to see that you can sometimes choose to let a mess sit while you jump to the aid of your team, but that you can also create space for yourself to clean that mess up. When your response is a calm, "It's okay, it's just dishes, they show up every day," you will train your team for things they can't find on a random training call or at any event. You train them on how to deal with life while pursuing success. In fact, that is success.

They want to see you dodge those bullets and duck the upper cuts life throws at you because it will make you better! When your tribe gets to look into the window of your life to see that it is occasionally chaotic and yet your chaos comes with beauty; when they see how it becomes more polished as the days pass, that's when your tribe will look in and say, "Yes, I do think I'd like to come in, too." Because this is a business that's built on the side with the little spare time we do have, to become the person we never had the chance to be.

If you are hiding your obstacles, you are doing your tribe and yourself a serious disservice. If you don't share your daily victories and your daily failures, and dancing with in them in all their glory, you are doing your team and yourself a serious disservice. If you're still in hiding, you are holding onto the lies that somehow you are all alone—telling yourself that you're not normal or worthy of having a voice. Then, my friend, you are doing yourself and others a serious disservice.

If you're standing in that lie of insecurity and the desire for perfection, then you're not breaking others free of that lie. You are holding the keys to freedom from yourself and from your friends. It's when we learn to live our life out loud and show the evolution in real time that others will know we can be trusted with their lives, too. That's when you really create freedom.

That's when the ranks and income will fall into place—and believe it or not, those victories will occasionally pale in comparison to everything else you had to overcome and learn to get there. And all that pressure you once felt between the two lives you're living will finally collide. But when you bounce back and push through instead of staying down, something beautiful happens that you could never have predicted. You break through and the pressure subsides, and suddenly, you're living life at a whole new level of comfort you had once only dreamed about.

From One Spark a Flame Can Ignite.

Don't be pushy with people's goals. My goals seven years ago were *so* ridiculously small in comparison to what we have created today. I wanted shopping money and to only help five people, and when someone tried to advise me differently, I shut them out.

Those goals were only small compared to now because as of today, over 20,000 lives have been assisted toward health because we said yes to my first small goal. Look, some people need time, credibility, and results to grow into different stages of goal setting. While we can ask questions to try to help people dig further to the core of their desires and potential achievements, we never want to belittle people's goals. Those first small goals just might be the benchmarks from which giants will grow.

"We never set goals for people, but rather it's our job to help you discover your goals and then give you action steps that we have proof will help you achieve those goals."

This is how we bring in all new partners into our organization. The only goal that matters to me is the goal of the person in front of me. One of the greatest gifts you can give yourself is the gift of no agenda. If you can truly be happy for people in whatever goal they set and whatever result they are okay with achieving, then you will truly be a leader that loves his or her whole team, no matter how much they earn or what rank they achieve. Help people win and you win, too. Who are you helping move forward today? Never stop being curious about who you can help next.

Things to Ponder

1. Remember: Know what you want for your future but then tuck it in your back pocket while you focus on helping others reach their goals.
2. Stars: Look for high quality partners: people who are respectful, kind, common values, strong marriages, and are looking for more. List a few.
3. Give and Receive: As you help your team achieve their goals, what are other ways these relationships can be of value in your life (outside of business growth)?

4. Grace under Fire: Don't shrink back when life gets messy. Rather, choose to get through the messy season in a new way and accept support so you can give support.

#COUNTINGSTARS

NINE

Recipe for Success

"You've got the music in you, don't let go. You've got the music in you, One dance left.
This world is gonna pull through. Don't give up. You've got a reason to live, can't forget . . . We only get what we give."
You Get What You Give ~ New Radicals

Are you following someone on the path to success? How incredibly grateful are you to have a role model in your life who has led with his or her actions to leave a trail of breadcrumbs to success?

Do you have a role model? I bet, if we really dig deep, there is an individual you admire. Maybe you admire this person from afar, having never met him or her and, perhaps, this person is very close to home.

Most often, admired people are people who achieved success in an area of their lives that is highly coveted. Sometimes, they are not people of financial success. In some cases, the person you admire might possess a beautiful marriage that is worthy of giving *The Notebook* a run for its money in the box office. Maybe your role model is a kind, peaceful person whose strength of faith and spirituality positively impacts everyone around them. Or perhaps, this person is a humanitarian, philanthropist, entrepreneur, athlete, or celebrity.

No matter the title or the accomplishment, I can assure you one thing: your role model followed in the footsteps of someone—likely several others. They, like the ones their role models followed, too, realized if there was knowledge to obtain it could be obtained from someone else who went before them. It's really not that complex of a thought.

If someone wants to be a doctor, he or she enrolls in college, then medical school, and residency. One seeks to learn from the best in their desired profession. If someone wants to transform their way of eating, they seek someone who has already created a personal transformation and has a wealth of knowledge to impart. Yet so many people (including us in the beginning) didn't really think we had much to learn or gain from others in our company or the industry.

Why would we, right? We didn't really respect network marketing as a legit industry. There are no degrees for network marketing and no schools to enroll in to learn this craft. Trust me, if you search, you can find the right role model and teacher in this industry, too.

. . .

An Unconventional Business Will Need an Unconventional Teacher

Ultimately, we learned that every ounce of our future success in our home-based business depended on this fundamental skill: duplication—a word often used in our industry, but not fully understood. It means to literally make a copy of something. Success in this industry (and in any area of life) requires us to literally mimic and copy those who were successful before us. It's so simple, and yet again, something people make so complicated. But why?

I know that in my past, I would often see individuals who possessed what I would consider partial success. There were people who were clearly wealthy beyond the scope of which any of us will ever experience, but they were on their fourth marriage, never saw their kids, and seemed to be empty despite their overflowing bank accounts. There was a part of their life I found amazing and yet, I did not want to duplicate the rest of their lives. That kind of success might come with long-term sacrifices I certainly was not willing to make.

On the other end of the spectrum, was my pride. We are all very unique individuals who possess different talents. Somehow, I assumed that if I mimicked others, I would lose credibility and creativity. It was as if I would become a clone. Or maybe I would face the mobs for not having created every single thing I did or said on my own. Oh, the shame!

Maybe this is not your issue, but it was a mountain for me until I learned the truth. The reason I was stuck was just because I was lacking the good common sense and business savvy of rinsing and repeating simple actions, teachings, and skills that had already been proven effective. It was also the reason our team was not growing. Duplication is a formula for success.

By taking systems proven efficient and making them your own, you start the process of repetition. If we can discover a system that is simple enough to be repeated over and over, that repetition can literally create new habits. Through painstakingly taking systems that you may not be comfortable with yet, and forcing yourself into a structure to do it anyway, you can to create comfort. What a novel concept. We must first become uncomfortable in order to become comfortable?

"Comfort is the enemy of progress."
P.T. Barnum

Yes, we must become uncomfortable to achieve results we have never experienced before. If we are going to look up to anyone and desire the life they have obtained, then we must be willing to do what he or she did to get there. We must get uncomfortable and learn new things to be the one who proves to others the system works when you're committed to duplicating success.

Repetition creates ownership. Take any skill—such as eating healthy daily for instance—and repeat it day after day, whether you make a mistake or have a holiday, and eventually you will possess a healthy body. Before you know it, eating healthy is just what you do and go back to, no matter what the situation or circumstance. If there is a system we can duplicate, then we can achieve results.

With time and work, we can rewrite our habits. Congratulations, through duplication, repetition, and grit, you have rewritten your DNA. There is no "sudden" transformation. No, the only kind of transformation that truly exists is an intentional transformation.

Breaking the Code

In your transformation lies the power for duplicate transformations. *That* is the power of network marketing. We unleash incredible potential and power through demystifying the keys to success. We humanize the business world and make it possible for anyone to walk through those doors using our own transformation as a beacon of hope. I don't know if you will, but I sure do hope you can grasp what I'm telling you.

Be the *rule* and not the exception, and others will follow you proudly.

You want to be a mirror for success. Here are a few simple areas in which you can show up well as a role model for your team:

- Company calls.
- Company events.
- Team calls or meetings.
- Social media.
- One-on-one mentoring.

- Lead from the front: personally building and growing.
- Build in a buffer for family time, personal time, and spiritual time.
- Prioritize your marriage.

Some people may be reading this, still holding onto this thought pattern, "But I have been on all the calls. I went to the events. I have heard it all." And I will ask you this, "You have heard it, but are you doing it *all* the time?"

My dear, dear friend, if you think you have heard and learned everything from a short season (and short may be a few weeks, few months, or even a few years) of investing your time, then I have news for you . . . You didn't.

Your brain will only absorb new content through hearing and doing. That means you can only absorb that which you actually do consistently. Additionally, there will be loads and loads of skills and actions your brain will not retain because we, as mere mortals, can only take action on a few things at one time. So go back to school. You're not there yet.

You have the right to build the culture you envision, but you don't need to reinvent the wheel to do so. Your business can be one built on integrity and good, sound, business ethics. And—surprise!—it will start with you. When you think about the new roots you wish to establish, the thriving, grateful team you wish to create, and you take full ownership, it will catapult you and others into success. You see, it's not about looking up your line to the person who has reached the top, expecting them to do the work for you just because they have the recipe for success. Rather, it's about you looking up the line and becoming a student of the person who has achieved success; that is actually doing your homework (and giving the answers to your team).

There is no specific rank that qualifies when one should start duplicating and modeling duplication for others. Duplication should kick in from the very moment you decide you're ready to be a leader and to create other leaders. Which is hopefully from the time you click "purchase" on your partnership.

Speaking of leadership, are you still feeling as though your mentor is supposed to be doing more for you? If so, please tell me now, in what area of business does it work like that? Can you go to the bank, get a business loan, open your own business, and then expect or demand to be partnered with another business owner to do the work of opening or running a business for you? Uh, nope.

It doesn't even work like that in a franchise. In a franchise, you invest money to use an established name, branding, and gather systems already done for you, but no one is going to open the doors for you. No one is going to do all of your marketing, make your social media posts, make or return phone calls, or clock in every day. No, building and running a business is up to you.

Open up your eyes. Network marketing is a business; it can almost be compared to a franchise with a few differences. Here you are your own boss. Here you can earn a passive income and have work location freedom. Here you are not held down by a corporation and you can actually be paid for mentoring and inspiring people to join your profession. You can get paid to help others achieve the first milestones you achieved that made such a big difference in your life.

The same things that made a big difference in your life and got your head above water will similarly help others. Yet, people are scared by others' concepts that network marketers are just trying to earn money off other people's work. In ignorance, people will often make the mistake of judging that which they don't fully understand. And unless you are a full-time earner in a direct sales company, I am sorry to tell you, but you don't know what our industry is about. The people judging you are not paying your bills, and they don't know your heart.

Furthermore, I will confide in you that we have spent many hours investing in others (our clients and partners), not getting paid in the forefront to be rewarded handsomely in the future. It was worth it. I have zero regrets from this business.

A Broken, Over-Glorified System

We have always worked hard at helping others. Even before joining this industry, we spent countless hours marketing, consulting, creating meal plans, conducting training sessions, boot camps, hiring employees, training employees, letting go of employees, and dealing with all the negativity. We broke our backs in our "real" business every single day and poured our energy into helping people achieve their health goals and into helping personal trainers start their careers.

What we received in return was a few good relationships and a whole lot of headaches. Often, we only trained up our future competitors and built them a client base with which they could leave us to move onto a different gym. Hold on as I get up on my soapbox!

Owning a small business is a broken system that often makes the business owner more of an employee than a business owner at all. That is not the kind of freedom that #freedomparents are looking for—just being their own employee, in debt to the bank, and in debt to employees. Small business owners are the first to be called when there is a problem, the first to fill in for sick employees, the last to make it home for dinner, the first missing their kid's firsts, the last to get paid, and the first to be dispensable to customers and employees for the next best thing.

It's a broken system that doesn't resemble the kind of freedom we all thought it would. We pour in our time, energy, and money and the return on investment is just barely what we think we deserve. The day I stood looking at the empty shell of what would be our soon-to-be gym, I envisioned it being the conduit to giving my family the world. I, like many other business owners, just was not aware of the other side.

In network marketing, energy, and knowledge you put in and pour into yourself and others can and will greatly compound over time. Every single interaction is an opportunity for growth. Even when things don't go as planned, those situations are simply lessons on how to mentor, who to work with, and where to grow. You can outgrow your mentors, which is never a possibility in a "real" business. You will never outgrow your boss in income, which is also why many employees leave. They, like you, seek opportunities to grow.

It's Enough to Make a Grown Man Cry

Do you remember when I told you about my breaking point? That day Harold came home broken. Being brought to tears was one of the worst and best moments in our life.

I always find it amazing how God can take our worst moments and turn them into one of the best moments. Silver linings really do exist.

A few months prior, we had one of the biggest losses at our business. Our lead trainer—the one who had been with us when the doors opened, the one we funneled client after client to for seven years; the one we trusted to open and close, the one we offered a franchise to, the one we placed in our marketing pieces, the one we trusted—he quit and took almost all of his clients—our clients—with him.

We could not fault any of them for doing what they did. He wanted to move on, and his next goals didn't include us. It was quite traumatic at the time, but now I am only thankful for that situation blowing up like it did. Our clients, well they didn't consider it an "ours" relationship. They trained in our facility, but their loyalty was with their trainer. As a fellow hustler, I get it. As a business owner with bills to pay, mouths to feed, and already under more stress than we could handle—in that moment we wanted to die a thousand deaths.

Drama after drama, we came to the powerful realization that our morals, work ethic, intentions, and integrity could never cut the cord that allowed these people to constantly pull our hours, our marriage, and our family into *their* agendas. If that business was our priority, then their agendas and issues would always be the center of our life. That's where I drew the line. My family, your family, should never, ever, ever be pulled into the Bermuda Triangle of other people's drama. We did not have to die on that hill and neither do you.

When people are given the opportunity to mimic success and offer it—rather than prescribe it—you are eventually living in the reality that you can create a voluntary army. An army of people who can share the same values, similar goals, and yet also be different at the same time. Independence and camaraderie are two things that most people crave; the ability to be wonderfully, uniquely you, plus the opportunity to have a community of people who lift you up rather than tear you down. It is a theory of allowing people to be dependent for a season while you empower them to be independent in the long run. Empowering people to be their own boss is a glorious system of self-mastery. And then the cycle just starts all over again. Rinse. Lather. Repeat. Rinse. Lather. Repeat. Duplicate. Empower.

Going BIG

We don't make people do things they are not empowered to do on their own. As you shine your light, your start will be True North for so many spectators who have enjoyed watching your show. Your evolution will be a sweet aroma that literally draws people into your world as a bee is drawn to honey. And don't try to be clever here. You can't just roll yourself in sugar to speed up the process. You have to transform from the inside out. It's a huge responsibility and honor. It is a role we must accept in humility as a servant leader; simply passing on the gifts we once unwrapped for ourselves.

As the numbers increase over time of the people you inspire, your next responsibility will be learning to discern who to work with, how to work with them, and how often. Many are called, but sadly, few are chosen. People will self-select. At first, it's so exciting to see that through changing your life and simply helping a few take steps forward in their lives, that your consistency and dedication can actually draw others in like a magnet. Then you will see that people will often raise their hands, truly desiring the results, but not ready to put the time or effort in to see results.

A leader must understand that we are advocates for other people's goals, but we can't wish them to be successful more than they desire it for themselves. You will have to learn to read people's actions more than their words. If you were to place every new or existing partner under a magnifying glass —to examine their goals, their lives, their words, and their actions—what does it tell you, the leader, that this person needs from you?

- A friend who checks in from time to time.
- A coach gently reminding them of their "why" and goals.
- A reminder to get into the safe-haven of team community as an incubator for growth and courage.

- An action-oriented checklist to keep on moving because the train is leaving the station!
- A leader to prepare the new leader for how to groom a large team.
- A leader looks into their team and tries his or her best to see past the fog and into clarity of what each individual really needs for growth.

Sometimes your partners will try to tell you what they need. Sometimes they are right, but they are also often wrong. Too often, people are scared of these new murky waters. They imagine it's unsafe as if a predator is lurking in the dark, ready to snap! They envision self-imagined danger that doesn't exist. A "Jaws" that is never going to strike. They want counseling. They want you to do the work for them rather than with them. You cannot build strong partners this way. Your key job as a leader is to empower people to uncover the power within. While we can get to know people, and you better—you cannot commit to weekly counseling. That is likely not on your resume, and if it is, it's not included here as your job requirement. But being a friend—you can do that. Plugging the team into weekly team meetings, a cocoon for self-improvement, you can do. You can provide a level of self-awareness through asking great questions, being curious, and letting your partner know he or she can pick up speed at any point he or she decides they're ready. Slow is good. Medium pace is good. Fast is good, too. Let them know the choice is up to them. Our greatest job is to help people make a commitment to their goals, responsibility, and taking action.

Heat-Seeking Missile

Every person comes into network marketing at a certain heat level. The higher their desire to grow, the bigger the *why*, the higher the heat level is on his or her thermometer. You will know it when you feel it. People who are *cold* will basically do nothing, but not forever—in some cases, they warm up.

Emotions don't matter here. I have heard some goals that brought me—and the other person—to tears, just for them to go home to do nothing. Often, these people are dealing with life situations, mindset issues, and confidence issues. Again, be a friend to these people, if they let you. They may not accept, but you can try to plug them into the community. They might warm up eventually, but don't sit around and wait. Keep on seeking heat. You might reach out to this individual once a month to let them know you are there for them. And always ask, "Are you ready to grow? How can I help you?"

Lukewarm. These are people who are doing something. It is wise to stay hip-to-hip with them and check in two or three times a month. Your touch points can go up as you watch their numbers, attendance, and communication levels. Sometimes, people who are lukewarm can heat up really fast, and sometimes it could take months or years, but I do notice that most of these people will be around for the long haul. It is so important to encourage them at every step. Celebrate them for actions, and celebrate the people they are helping as your partner takes the time to become clear on what it is he or she wants from their business and for their team. So many of these individuals just need a little time to cook. I am never surprised when they eventually grow into full-blown leaders.

!Muy Caliente! That's "very hot" in Spanish, in case you're wondering. Look out, because this partner is on fire. Their *why* is strongly connected to their desire for growth and freedom. But the secret sauce lies in the fact that the person sees so clearly that they have a vehicle for creating freedom and all they need to do, is stay in massive action! Your job is to help them do just that!

You keep passing the ball as they pass it back to you. This is a game of catch, and every time you throw the ball back to this person, it is with a new action step. Just as much as you want to lace up your running shoes and just run side-by-side with this partner, you are also going to model to them how to pull out the slippers and PJ's and just chill.

We will have to help them manage their disappointments because high achievers can be very hard on themselves. We must encourage them to take time to breathe and celebrate their victories, otherwise, this person could be so inclined to work themselves into the ground. Burnout is a real thing in any profession. Since we can work our business anytime from anywhere, it's critical for us to learn and to teach others to stop and enjoy the roses.

To be a leader, we must have keen senses. It can be so difficult to understand that we are not superheroes. No amount of capes and masks will turn us into heros who can drag limp bodies across the finish line. To the person who is not used to working with people, this can be frustrating and saddening. We don't want to leave anyone behind, but there are some people who actually just want to be left behind. I know, it's sad. It breaks my heart a little every day until I look at the people who are actually pulling themselves into the life raft and waving their arms with all ferocity screaming: "Here, here, I am ready! Give me my oar."

It was a Facebook post that brought us one of our fastest-growing partners today. Well, to be honest, it was a series of posts, but there was one post in particular that threw this guy over the ledge to where he had to know what we're doing for a living.

In this video post, Harold was tearing up his student loans. We were debt-free. Not only were we debt-free, but we were living and working on our terms and taking extended trips and vacations. Our friend was caged by a high-stress sales job that provided a decent income. He was close to earning six figures a year. But he saw we had something he didn't: work- and life-purpose, fulfillment, and flexibility. Our friend came to us already knowing what he wanted, and with no shame or doubt, he looked at us and said, "I want what you have."

Now, many may say these things, but few will actually honor it. Too many allow fear to get in the way. This guy didn't. Johnny simply trusted us and the process immediately from day one and applied massive action. Seven months later, his then full-time gig went into sudden layoffs. What could have been an extremely stressful moment was one of actual blessing for our partner because he had already replaced that income with his side hustle. Work with the willing and watch that rising tide raise all the ships around it.

<u>We can only work with the working</u>. A leader has to learn how to manage your time and emotions, otherwise, you will

blink your eyes and realize you allowed someone who isn't ready for growth to steal your focus from someone who is. This happened to me four years ago.

I stood in my kitchen at the end of a long day and saw a Facebook notification that I was on probation for twenty-four hours. Ouch! Facebook jail is not fun in our profession. But, why? I never sent spammy messages or friend people that I shouldn't in excessive numbers. I was blocked and reported. Suddenly, I received a firestorm of messages and emails from a former partner. She was angry at herself and fearful, but she decided to fire at me. I was so hurt and upset. All I could do was go back and forth with this person to try to calm her down and see how I could help her. But nothing I said could smother her rage. I blinked, and four hours of my life disappeared just like that. I had allowed myself to be caught in her web.

I lost four hours of my life with my kids and my husband trying to help someone who didn't want my help. Now, this is a rare outburst. I don't think many people will encounter such a situation, nor have I since. You will encounter passive aggressiveness, silence, people who sign up with other opportunities and even other distributors. You will encounter people who gave up on themselves. Those people are the ones who are saying "Yes, help me," while their heads are actually shaking no. But that truth hurts too much, so it's easier to blame you, your company, or any warm body in front of them.

As long as you have acted in integrity, it's not about you; it's about them. If you did indeed do what you were supposed to do, then all you can do is choose your reaction (or lack thereof) and just move on with kindness. Immediately turning to the ones you are helping and those who do appreciate you and douse those flames with more fuel.

I wish I would have immediately ignored her messages that day, and just thanked God for him keeping me off of social media and gifting me with the opportunity to call my client who had lost over a hundred pounds, or my partner who just hit her first big business milestone. When people mean to harm you, simply pull yourself into your happiness. Go celebrate someone who values you. Play with your kids and hug your spouse. Count all the ways you are helping people. Don't allow yourself to be pulled into the lie. You are a world-changer starting with your world first, and then others.

Leadership isn't easy, but easy is overrated. Nothing worth having in life is easy. On the path to becoming a leader, you will find great time freedom, financial freedom, the ability to create a legacy of freedom for others behind you; but by far one of the best gifts we received from leadership is the gift of peace of mind in any situation. That's also worth duplicating to others. So seek the fires! Look for people with that spark in their eyes. Speed of implementation is a skill we must all learn and seek. If we operate on the same mundane to-do list and nothing is ever checked off, that is not speedy implementation. Learn to give yourself, and others, no more than one to three actionable items at a time. When those are completed, we can add more.

Step-by-step we amaze ourselves because we are actually getting things done! Step-by-step we are amazed by others, because they are actually getting things done. How we communicate and work with ourselves will transcend into how we communicate and work with others. If we decide to stay downtrodden and pulled down, then we will only accidentally encourage others to focus on negativity. If we choose—in any situation—to rise up above the negativity to seek positivity and growth, we can do the same for others. To become a leader, we must choose to become a leader before the title. The rank is just a pleasant confirmation you are on your way, and the income a subtle reward for relentless efforts. Leadership is this beautiful concoction of personal evolution with a dose of hope and a splash of legacy, gently stirred—not shaken. Don't just try to throw it back like a college frat boy would; it will knock you off your feet, and you'll wake up with a hangover. Sip it casually and often and let the euphoria sink in over time.

"Don't fight it, it's coming for you, running at ya
It's only this moment, don't care what comes after
Your fever dream, can't you see it getting closer?
Just surrender 'cause you feel the feeling taking over
It's fire, it's freedom, it's flooding open."

The Greatest Show - The Greatest Showman

Things to Ponder

1. Question: Are you still winging it?

2. Coachable: Who in your business is an example of success you can model?
3. Truth: Are you constantly caught in someone else's agenda?
4. Energy Management: Work with the working people who are action takers.

#RECIPEFORSUCCESS

TEN

The Freedom Frontier

"Had to have high, high hopes for a living. Shooting for the stars when I couldn't make a killing. Didn't have a dime, but I always had a vision. Always had high, high hopes."
High Hopes ~ Panic at The Disco

Why is music intertwined throughout this story? Music was once my only escape. As my feet pounded on the pavement and the music beat in my ears, it seemed to make up for the lost beats of my heart.

A stroller in front of me carrying my most prized possessions, my two daughters, music kept my heartbeat strong for those two pieces of innocence in front of me. They, my carrots, guided this tired workhorse one step further, one foot in front of the other.

Music was my friend. It was the kind, forgiving friend who

wrapped me in a hug no matter how I presented myself that day. It was also the friend who allowed me to get my anger out and hit my feet on the pavement like a punching bag.

Music was my visionary, too. It was the kind of charismatic friend who lights up a room and has the ability to travel with you through time into the future. Music helped me see the future I once struggled to see.

During a certain space of time, I questioned whether there was really anything I was worthy of doing anymore. I had pictured so much for my life, and only three of those things had come true, and two of them were falling apart (my marriage and business). The rest of my life seemed to be an obscure, blurry vision that held little promise.

People who knew me then and still now, would never know truly the depths of my despair in this short, yet excruciatingly long, phase of my life that I quite honestly couldn't wait to see finished. There were times that life was so hard and the future so uncertain that I questioned if maybe my husband was better off without me. I questioned if my daughters were better off without me. I questioned if the world was better off without me.

But there were other forces fighting for me. There's a force fighting for all of us. I chose to listen closely. Some days, David Bowie himself reassured me by helping me understand the immense pressure we were under as young adults, a young married couple, and young parents. We were still just babies coming into the world with such a heavy load on our shoulders. It was a weight we were not strong enough to hold alone or all at once.

And then, my girl, Tracy Chapman, would chime in; she

would remind me of our earlier years together when we had just fallen in love. She would remind me of riding in Harold's red Mustang, her song playing, and Harold and I would say at the same time, "I love this song!"

Suddenly—on a day when I felt like we had nothing in common, and I didn't know if I knew the man in front of me—I would remember that he was the one who wanted to get out of that small-town way of thinking with me. In his fast car, we could get away to anywhere we wanted, *if* we wanted.

When I thought our marriage was falling apart, and that I was utterly worthless, capable only of bringing our glorious children into this world, I just wanted to give up. I felt like a failure every day, other than the days I gave birth to my daughters. Something would whisper to me, "Keep your eyes open, my love." It was almost as though God whispered that through my iTunes. It was literally these messages sent into the world that saved my life—like a rope thrown out into the unknown. I was the one to see it and grab onto it. Some days, it pulled me up so high that I felt as though I could fly. Other days, it nudged me to trudge on, because I was loved and I was needed. On many days, music was my shoulder to cry on.

This might seem like a far stretch, but I believe that life is beautiful like that. In our hardest, darkest, weakest times; God will insert His beauty, peace, and hope.

The playlist I have listened to over and over again to write this book is the same playlist that I have listened to for seven years. The tears I cry as I listen to them now are tears of undying gratitude. The fact is that, when they first entered my ears all those years ago, I had no idea what each song was exactly trying to tell me or what it would mean to me in the future. Listening to them now, I can only smile. Their prophetic words sunk into my heart and perpetuated into our entire life. They tell a story of suffering, surrender, curiosity, trust, diligence, faith, love, mending, confidence, and courage. These songs freed me when I was still a prisoner in my own life.

There was a time I wanted to disappear. But I fought it. Just listening to my music and running around my neighborhood no longer felt like I was running away from my problems for a day. Those stinking problems kept finding me—and they became quicker and smarter than me. I could not stand the skin in which I was living. I was not fulfilled in the business in which I thought I would find unending fulfillment. I was done feeling like a failure. And I no longer wanted to take my family down in the debris of a storm I refuse to confront. I had every reason to be happy and grateful and yet, something told me that there was still more out there for me and my family. But I was already tired, exasperated, and felt as though I was failing. How could I possibly be capable of creating anything more than what I had already done? I just did not see it.

My second daughter, Mila, was ten months old as postpartum depression hit me like a ton of bricks. It collided with the very real stress of our financial distress and my emotional distress. I worked all the time, but I slept very little and ate even less. I felt completely selfish for being so tormented, which only made matters worse. My life was spinning so fast and all its jagged edges were ripping me apart. Worst yet, I knew my husband felt the same; neither of us were happy.

The internal turmoil turned into external turmoil I could no longer ignore. As my thoughts became darker and darker late one night, a familiar feeling came over me. One that I hadn't felt in years. A feeling I was not happy to recall. I wanted to give up. I wanted to be erased from this world. I looked down at my left wrist. The scar there is faint, but the pain still very real. The confusion and hopelessness of that moment was all too real, and I remembered the very poor choice I almost made when I was seventeen years old.

It would have been the worst decision ever to take my own life. I came to that realization too many years ago as my little sister stood outside that door crying. I didn't do it the "right way" as some would say. The scar on my wrist is horizontal and not vertical. There was a part of me that day that just couldn't stand myself, my life, and the feelings I couldn't understand. Nonetheless, I wanted to be gone for the mere fact that I wanted to matter. I wanted people to miss me. I wanted my existence to be known no matter how short-lived it might be.

As the blade cut deeper into my fragile teenage skin and I sobbed knowing every single movement drew me closer to really making the most final decision of my life—I suddenly stopped. Out of my total darkness, I felt a light within. In an instant, I knew that I was loved, and that I mattered. Instantly, my heart switched from a lifeless victim into warrior mode. I dropped the blade, wrapped a bandage around my wrist, walked out that door and hugged my sister as I begged her for forgiveness and vowed to her that I would never ever go into such a severe place of self-loathing. I vowed to always and forever be a child of the light.

You might imagine that my family noticed the bandage on my wrist or that they got me help right away. They didn't. Till now, only my sister, Blythe, and my husband know about that day. And it was for good reason. That incident would bring me no glory and no glory to God. But my survival and ability to thrive in such a miraculous way would.

So when I felt that feeling coming over me once again, there was not even a thought in my mind that I should not fight back. I reached out to one of the few people I knew I could trust with such a delicate matter; my sister, Elisha. Her words saved me that night. "Samantha," she said, "the only thing wrong with you is that you're not taking care of you."

She was right. I chose a cycle of self-defeat. I was hunting it down because to fall into that pattern of self-loathing was my fix. Broken and unfulfilled started to become my identity. I wished I had asked her how she knew. How she could possibly understand the void that was my life at that time? When I stood in that hospice house with her, I finally understood. Despair, boredom, and desiring a purpose-driven life is not a mental illness; it is an affliction that sets in with adulthood. We are all living our own versions of a storm that refuses to settle.

Look, your life may be pretty ridiculously blessed, but if you are feeling the itch to elevate yourself to the next level of being for whatever reason, you better go ahead and scratch. That itch will never just fade away.

Some of us can just numb the nagging pain and drown out the voices. Our families provide us with a beautiful purpose. As our internal chaos wrecks us, so does that storm tend to wreck the structures surrounding us. The storm that chases us, pulls others into the winds. Quite simply, if we don't become happy just being in pursuit, then our loved ones will have to watch while the person they know and love becomes a pale, unfulfilled less-familiar version of what he or she once was. That is not a burden your children, spouse, friends, or you should ever have to carry.

While people, including yourself, stand on the side-lines, dumbfounded by our uneasiness, they will try to politely nudge you back in the direction you are trying to change:

"Provide for your family," they tell us.

"You're lucky you can pay the bills," we tell ourselves.

The suggestion that we must just make due with making due is boring and unsettling. Eventually, the drudgery wears someone down. Years later, people will jump in to defend the older, worn out version of who we've become because, "We always worked so hard."

I didn't do what most level-headed people do—which would be consulting a physician and getting on medication—which I strongly advise you do if you need to. Please, seek professional help, because many of us just need as many people in our corner as we can get.

I, on the other hand, made the very risky choice of refusing to take that conversation any further that night. Even if medication were fit for that very difficult scenario in my mind that night, I don't know if I would have accepted it. I had seen my mother, sisters, and friends in similar situations. I have been a child of a medicated household for as long as I could remember and I had seen it help no one further than numbing their pain temporarily or turning into an addiction. Medication may have prolonged their lives, but it did not improve their lives. I did not want to numb this pain; I wanted to eradicate it. The truth is that I never wanted to end my life, but rather, I just wanted to live the life I knew I was meant to live. I wanted to live the life I was being too cowardly to live.

So, I sought to mend the very things that were causing my heart to ache and took me further away from the life I was meant to live. I sought to find a career that would allow me to be a mother and my husband to be a father. I sought to find a career that would bring out the leader within. I sought out a career that would allow me to empower others as I mended myself; one that would make me come from a place of integrity. I sought a life of adventure outside of my cozy suburban life. I sought a life free of shackles that we could fall madly in love with because that's what I needed to feel alive. And we dared to think that we were not alone; that there were others who needed to know they could seek the kind of freedom for their families that would have them turn to the mirror every single day and say at least one point or another, "I LOVE my life!" We chose to climb daily mountains to transcend the view in our very own home, so we could live a life of purpose to live on purpose with our kids. That mountaintop view from the flatlands of Mandeville, Louisiana, would eventually turn into real-life mountain views in Arizona, y'all!

The truth is, many people can admit they are stressed, worried about their finances, or just plain tired, but very few of us will admit the depth of which that pain travels. It's not until you hit the lowest of lows that, in the midst of that sorrow, can we decide to feel every ounce of the emotions attempting to lead us to a resolution. It's not until a friend calls you and says in tears, "I have a new *why*. I need to take some of this financial burden off of my husband's shoulders."

My friend and partner in business called and confided in

me as her friend—but also humbly, her business coach—that there was a deeper goal she was hiding. Her husband called 911, thinking he was having a heart attack. But it was merely a panic attack brought about by the immense burdens of his fatherly responsibilities. It took her six months to admit that they were under this kind of stress. Did you really think you were the only one?

See, I knew I was a mentally stable person being shaken by the unstable world around me. All I needed to do was reach out and grab the lifeline. I was tormented as a failure because I knew I was indeed no failure. I felt disconnection in a career of my own design and it was time to design a new career. I questioned the life I lived because it was not the life our family was really meant to live.

I dare you to question the unquestionable and to be unsettled by the settled life, and through the darkness of those questions, I hope you find a brilliant light of answers. Through challenging myself to question what the definition of happiness would be for my family, I found solutions that would not only act as a Band-Aid for my wounds but also cure me of that disease. It was the search for an antidote, if you will.

If it Bothers You, it's Born in You

There was a nagging in me that I couldn't ignore. If I tried to ignore it, even more chaos ensued in its path. Are you living an unsettled life? The truth is, I could have survived changing nothing. Would I be as happy and as evolved as I am today? Probably not. Because there was something else, another purpose for me in this world, planted in me before I became a wife, gym owner, and mother. But that's my story.

I can't tell you what you need or give you the answers to living your most fulfilled life. No one could truly give that to me either. I found hope in the form of a direct sales opportunity that encouraged me to live my most optimal life in all facets. I had no other option but to trust in complete evolution through surrendering to that process because the company supported my core values. As I trusted and followed a trail of success, licking up every little breadcrumb I could, my belly would be full for once, my heart a little lighter, and my resume a little stronger.

Had I turned away from that opportunity, life would have gone on in another path, just as it did for my parents and for my siblings. As several of my siblings faded away from this world, I can't help wondering; if they had seen my parents move on to their higher calling, would they have been the beneficiaries of a higher courage of their own? If our house wasn't divided because my father had to pay the bills the only way he knew how—would the children in my home have grown up feeling a little less alone?

I look at my own children and envision them as grown adults, too, and living in the same confusion in which I used to live. I could not bear picturing them as myself. When I looked into my children's eyes, I knew that they needed to see me, us, actually go through this transformation. Sabella, Mila, and Stellan needed to know they could evolve and change course at any time. They could discover new paths because they saw their parents do it. We changed to give our children the permission to change, too.

My father did achieve success within his full-time job. He went from being an offshore electrician on an oil rig to creating computer programs and administrative systems at the corporate office in Houston without going back to college or receiving any formal schooling. When he finally retired, he proudly showed me one of the largest sums of money I personally had ever seen in one check at that time. I was one of the few he could show.

My mother was bedridden, and my siblings were going through their own battles. Instead of using that money—as planned—to travel the world with my mother in retirement, he used it for hospital stays and her funeral. Instead of funding weddings, he funded a divorce and three of his seven children's funerals. I was proud of him for having achieved his vision, if not at least in part. But I know for him it was only bittersweet, because somewhere along the way, several of his children, the people he loved most, became lost in the woods.

My father, my mother, my husband, and I aren't the first parents to hang our heads in remorse of what we know we couldn't give our children, and unfortunately, we won't be the last. But maybe, just maybe, together we can free at least one. Maybe we will become the tribe that reaches out our hands and at least offers freedom to parents who are seeking it. That cage I used to live in; I didn't want to stay there. I didn't have to either because someone in 2012 reached out and offered me a solution. Maybe not the one anyone thought I needed, but it surely was the keys to freedom, nonetheless.

#FreedomFrontier

ELEVEN

Call It a COMEBACK

"They say it's all been done, but they haven't seen the best of me. I have one more run and it's gonna be a sight to see."
High Hopes ~ Panic at the Disco

Chapter after chapter, I have taken you through our past in order to be in the present with you. I have opened my heart to you to hold space for you in this moment, knowing that, in you, there is also is a Freedom Parent begging to come out. I hope that you can see you are not alone.

But, nine chapters later, I no longer want to talk about the past. I want to talk about the future. A future so sweet that as many times that I have fallen to my knees crying in despair, tenfold over I have fallen to my knees in utter joy and amazement over the bliss that our life has turned into.

In church, songs of praise draw more tears that wash my soul clean. These tears fall from my eyes week after week. Even my tears have transformed in the midst of the peace and power that we intentionally crafted into our lives during this process. We really did find our strength in our weakness!

There are new songs added to my old playlist now. I don't aim to live in the past. Our past is a powerful teacher that leaves us with lectures of love and lessons of liberty. I aim to honor my past, for without it, we would not be where we are today. As we honor the past, we actively pull our future forward. Because we don't get bitter, we get better. The new songs on my iTunes playlist celebrate the freedom we live today. They sing of glory, love, and resurrection.

My family dances, we sing, and we celebrate the Freedom Parents that have emerged because we dared to accept the challenge to redefine our life several years ago. One by one the stories unfold, the messages flood in, and sure enough, other people that were afflicted by the same dysfunction, lethargy, and broken financial states are emerging as butterflies, too. They thank us for being crazy enough to say yes to a simple opportunity so they could, in turn, say yes, too. They thank us for making them believe that they could define what their #FreedomFamily would be and how they would live.

But all we can do is thank them for trusting as we trusted years ago when we were still broke and broken.

I, once on the verge of divorce, am married to a man I have been blessed to fall in love with not just once, but twice. I watched his metamorphosis into the beautiful creature I always knew he was in the first place. He has turned into the fearless leader of our team and the voice of wisdom and discernment for those who wish to learn from our success. Harold, after all, is my biggest encourager who gladly stepped in that role for my mother and eagerly cheers for me with my father.

He celebrates my crazy hare-brained ideas and even plants a few himself. I speak a dream, and he launches it. He knows my heart, and he protects it with such courage that his own discomfort is not enough to scare him.

In February 2018, he propelled another one of my childhood dreams into existence. For two years, we had been looking at future homes in a mountain landscape, because I was in love with the mountains from my childhood adventures with my parents. Harold, a nature lover, was a proponent, but honestly, I think he also could have settled for a vacation home. Leave it to a woman to push a man over the edge.

But I kept telling him, "Harold, for just once in my life, I want to experience what it's like to live outside of Louisiana. I don't want to live and die in this one corner of the world." For some reason, I desperately needed to experience a long-term move. So, when we visited Arizona in December of 2017, on a business trip, he took it out of the virtual world and scheduled tours of homes there.

We boarded our plane to return to New Orleans, and not long after the plane ascended into the air, Harold turned to me and said, "Let's do it. Let's move."

I said ecstatically, "YES!" and laid my head back on the chair and thought to myself, "Wow, who has this man become?"

Three months later, we would move halfway across the U.S. together; our first-ever move out of state, possibly only because we simply had the emotional freedom, time freedom, and financial freedom to finally do so.

My children who were once second to the paycheck—because we had no other option—are now the priority and the purpose that fuels the paycheck. We tuck them in at night, drop them off at school, and pick them up daily. There are days when I find myself telling Harold, "You know, you can just take the kids to school today. We don't need to both go," and then, three minutes later, I'm running frantically out to the car anyway because, why not? My kids always say, "Mommy, I thought you were staying home?" to which I reply, "I'll start work soon, baby, after I walk you into class."

We take days off just because, and together we are living out dreams that I once could only imagine as a child. Together, we take horseback riding, Spanish lessons, have talks about our future two-month adventure to Spain, and we explore topics for their first book, should they want to write it.

As we approach their teen years—years that I remember being so fragile—we have been intentional about making sure all our daily choices, business or not, are surrounded by the fact that we should create a relationship with them now if we want to stand any chance of being a voice of reason when they will need us most—when they emerge into adulthood themselves.

Call it crazy, but I believe we must earn the right to be the loving voice in our children's heads guiding them back home through the dark and into the light. It's not enough for us to just be close in space with our children. We must create space each day for them in which their parents are fully present, our minds free from clutter, confusion, and chaos. Our career is no longer only about affording opportunities for our children so that they can have a better life than we had. We don't clock in our best hours to only bring money into our home. Our career is about creating a better life for the whole family, including the parents; a life we can live right here and right now.

You don't have to sacrifice yourself for the sake of your children. You were given this one life so you can live it in full joy, passion, and purpose, too. Were you not once a child? Take care of that child, too.

Don't just attempt to be the lesson; be the rule. Don't beg your children to write a chapter you yourself refused to complete. Sit down, dig deep, and write out your story, the way it was meant to be told. The real story. You know, that story you dug a hole for and buried years ago—go dig it up. But, make no mistake of labeling it.

I wanted to be a neurosurgeon and Harold an international businessman. When we decided to call off our previous career, we never thought this path would actually get us to the place we desired most. No, I'm not going to tell you I'm now in medical school, but rather I'm doing what I wanted to do when I attached the label "doctor" as the method of getting there; I am helping people, a lot of people. And Harold? Well, in 2019, as our company expands to the Asian markets, he will become an international businessman. In retrospect, listening to the depth of our unhappiness and actually doing something about it, was the exact path we were meant to follow.

The people I love ignited a dream in me. The stars that I

gaze upon shined bright enough that I could see the light within myself. When my husband and I learn to draw closer to each other daily, we learn to draw the parts of the world that we choose into us. We work so hard at living our best life because we know that it is the only way to prepare for setting our children free. We are learning how we can do a better job of calmly drawing our children closer to us so we can one day gently push them out into the world. So they, in their own time, can draw into themselves what the world means to them. This enables them to define their purpose through the ebb and flow of life. They can stop at any point in their lives and leave behind what is no longer acceptable to step into the next evolution.

The Eye of the Storm

We parent our children from a place of confidence. We mentor our team from a place of courage. We speak out our mission into the world from a place of purpose. Before we could do any of this, we first had to step into the storm. Look, we know a thing or two about a storm. Growing up in Louisiana near the Gulf and Lake Pontchartrain, every single year that we lived there, all the residents, including us, held our breaths in expectation of the storm or storms of the season. If you chose to live there it is just a reality you learn to live with. If the storm is large enough, you evacuate (if you can afford to), or if it's a category one or two or a tropical depression, you might stay and take your chances. Either way, a safe-haven is not guaranteed. When those winds pull you in, you have no option but to give in to the storm and what it decided to do with you, your home, and your family.

Hurricane Katrina was proof of that. We evacuated, but many stayed. Many helpless people lost their lives, their homes, and their security. We all rebuilt. New Orleans is as bustling as ever today, but it does not come without paying the price to the storm.

We will all go through our own storms in life. You can continue to run and experience constantly bumping into the outer-bands of those thunderous winds, only ever escaping long enough to pull yourself back together until it strikes again next season. Or you can decide to charge head first into the storm and make it your own; to let it chisel away at all the things about your life that are no longer essential. To lose the dead weight that is holding you down. As you charge forward, you get to the eye of the storm which, without those ferocious winds, could not exist. Those disastrous winds and black clouds pull back to reveal the calm of the storm. The quiet, the light, the peace—until the winds pass back over you, like a train charging right at you. You will be sucked back into the storm, but look, I'm telling you now, keep charging forward. Keep fighting for the calm.

When the winds rise up again, run forward as fast as you can to take back the eye of the storm until that storm passes for good. I like to think we name Hurricanes after people for a good reason. There is nothing more powerful, resilient, and regenerative as a revival that comes after a collapse. Storms and people can cause just as much damage, but as we can produce so much damage, we are also as capable of resurgence.

Let's face it, y'all, humans can create quite a mess, and somehow, we still manage to make that mess beautiful. We are capable of a comeback. And, just by working through the comeback, you will naturally come back stronger. The calm of the storm could not exist without those ferocious all-consuming winds. Without the heat, the climbing pressure, and the torrential downpour that swells up, the storm would not exist. But would any of us be any better for never ever having experienced the storm? Would we be able to appreciate the sunshine on our faces had we never been lost in the dark? Would we be able to relax in a cool sweet breeze, had we not been almost swept away by it?

I, for one, appreciate my days far more now, knowing that once I questioned if I should be gifted more. I cherish each moment with my kids, knowing my sisters' children miss them dearly. Because I miss my sisters and brother dearly myself, I work harder to get my message out into the world for the ones who need to hear it. I celebrate every single dollar that enters our bank account, because it's earned by doing work we down-right love, while working with people we would fight back-to-back with any day. But it's also a career that gifts us with the most valuable gift of all: time.

I'm no longer waiting for a battle so that I can enjoy my life. I appreciate my life, having been through the battles. By going through the battle dead-set on winning, we have found a victory. Look y'all, I am not looking to die another day. I am looking to live another day and another and another so long as God gifts us with the ability to walk this Earth with a purpose. I am not naïve enough to say my battling days are over, but I am done looking for battles that don't need to be fought.

However, there is the unresolved case of your freedom. *Here my friend, take my sword and use it. Use it with courage! Be fierce and fight to soar, and by all means, don't you dare stop swinging until you find your family's BIG break!*

I believe that we are all entitled to the same human rights. Rights to explore, travel, evolve, love, empower, surrender, and conquer. All of which we must first attempt on ourselves, and then we can share with the world. Build your tribe, free your family, and create financial abundance beyond your wildest dreams. It all might just happen for you through the odd vehicle of a tiny little direct sales opportunity.

Your voice matters, from the point at which you decide that *you* matter. Shine your light, dance to your music, and may your goals and dreams steer you and many others toward the #FreedomFrontier. Rise above, my friend, and run ahead as fast as you can. And don't look back until you're proud of all you have created. Because there is a comeback waiting for you and, oh boy, y'all, it is gonna be good!

"You and I, we're not tied to the ground.
Not falling, but rising, like rolling around.
Eyes closed above the rooftops . . .
Eyes closed, we're gonna spin through the stars.
Our arms wide as the sky.
We gonna ride the blue all the way to the end of the world. To the end of the world.
And when the kids are old enough, we're going to teach them how to fly."

SAMANTHA AND HAROLD LEE PRESTENBACH

You and Me ~ Dave Matthews Band

#THECOMEBACK

TWELVE

Manhood, Fatherhood & Fulfillment

W hat side of ridiculous are you living on? We all are living in one of these worlds—whether it be the world of ridiculously struggling to get by, or in the world of living a ridiculously blessed, abundant life. The beautiful thing is that we all have a choice of which side we want to live on. Sure, it will take some work, and rest assured, it will be difficult at times . . . But if we are to be honest here, I (it's Harold speaking here, if you haven't caught on) have been on both sides, and I have found that I'd much rather have a difficult day striving for a life of abundance than a difficult day of struggling just to survive . . . Do you feel the same way?

All Things Leave an Impression

I can recall, as a child, watching my grandpa, uncles, and my father all illustrate to me what hard work looked like. They all had a very strong work ethic. I've never known my father not to have a job or two. They all were reliable, loyal individuals to their chosen craft and companies. It was what I saw as normal and would later mimic. They all adopted a trade, and they worked it five, six or sometimes seven days a week from dawn to dusk. Don't get me wrong; they seemed to really love their crafts and the people they worked with. Their jobs became their identity. Grinding it out, and commuting hours a day to and from work just to survive and slide into Friday evening exhausted, became their lives. Sometimes they only enjoyed a restful Saturday and maybe half of a Sunday. I say half because they had to mentally prepare for the Monday grind to begin again, leaving Sunday afternoon off limits.

Like many people, they had become slaves to health insurance and one-to-two-week paid vacations a year. They were caught in the invisible prison of mediocrity, and they had no idea they were trapped in it. Granted, they were really good at what they did, and I'm pretty sure the "work" itself they enjoyed immensely. They were all respected by their colleagues for how well they performed at their jobs. But at what cost? They had no idea. Perhaps some of this resonates with your current or past situation?

I remember working with my father and uncle when out for summer breaks and holidays. I would wake up super early, commute miles, clock in, clock out, commute home, shower, eat, fall asleep in front of the TV, only to wake up and repeat, simply counting down the days to my weekend fishing trip or a night out. I can remember working in some office buildings in New Orleans and seeing sharply dressed, well-groomed gentleman walking around, laughing and appearing to be enjoying their day. They seemed respected, educated, and have more purpose and enjoyment out of what they were doing. They drove nice vehicles and just had an attractive presence to them that caught my attention. The seed was planted.

Because of that impression, I would go on to college and still work the summers with my family in construction. But in my mind, it was only temporary. I would be the one working to rise above all of it.

I'm sure you know the feeling. Perhaps you were unsure as to which proverbial vehicle out of college would take you there, but you knew life would be better. Often, my family encouraged and bragged about me for striving for a college education in hopes of obtaining a white-collar job. After all, that's what a college degree does, right? It guarantees you your dream job that delivers you the proverbial white picket fence, three kids, a beautiful wife, living happily ever after into the sunset . . . or does it? Now, I'm sure your "dream life scenario" looks a little different, but you get my drift.

So, the day has come. I have arrived . . . I have my degree, and an offer I accepted from a Fortune 400 company. Life was great; it was actually fantastic. I had thought, "Laissez le bons temps rouler," as we say in Louisiana, which means, "Let the good times roll." My starting salary as a "manager in training" was $32,000 with seven days' paid vacation, paid holidays, health insurance, and a matching 401K. Say what!? I was the man and moving on up, so to speak. My parents were super proud, Sam (who was my girlfriend at that time) was impressed, her parents were impressed, and—boom!—life was great. So I thought . . .

. . .

Enter Reality

I can recall arriving at my training store on Day One, all dressed up in my clean pressed pants, clean starched button-up shirt, ready to conduct some business. There was definitely a little swagger in my stride. With my chest puffed up, I couldn't help but think again, "Yeah, I am the man."

I could remember the staff sort of snickering when I walked in, but I had no idea what that was about. However, it soon dawned on me. What seemed quickly and abruptly was around three hours later. I found myself in the middle of a war zone. Literally, all hell broke loose.

The morning rush of contractors came in like a tsunami, looking to destroy everything in its path. Customers, coworkers —everyone seemed to be spitting orders at me non-stop. I can remember very distinctly retreating to the restroom at lunch and hiding in there, covered in sweat, filthy, and thinking, *What the hell just happened?* I felt like I was in the corner after fighting a few rounds with a heavyweight boxer.

Yep, I got my teeth bashed in that day, but more tragically, my ego was destroyed that day, too. I remember commuting a very long one hour home (yep, I unknowingly adopted the family commute) and thinking, *How could this be?*

This had to be a mistake. I was supposed to be laughing, having lunch with colleagues at nice restaurants. You know, enjoying my job. After a night's rest and recovering from my Day One wounds, I recall commuting back the next morning. This time, I was more mentally prepared for what the day would potentially throw at me. I convinced myself not to fret as I simply needed to learn the ropes from the bottom and work my way up. I remember thinking, *You got this, HP.*

Surely, things would improve as I became more competent and better at what I was doing. I had a great training manager who was a by-the-book micromanager kind of guy. At times, he got on my nerves if we are to be honest, but over time, I realized it was like the karate kid and Mr. Miyagi. His micromanaging conditioned and taught me to become a really good manager; so good that I received the opportunity to choose my own store to manage. In return, I started to earn more, which meant increased responsibilities.

As I was working my way up to that plush corporate office in the sky, I would later go on to earn the highest sales awards the company offered two years in a row. Earning me two trips to Hawaii at the ripe old age of twenty-four and twenty-five. I also earned the opportunity to choose my second store to manage, and it was a much larger volume branch and also closer to my home. This, I must say, was the most enticing, because ultimately, deep down, I desired and valued more time. And although this location didn't feel right, it would cut my commute in half. And let's face it, who enjoys extra commute time?

So I took it on, and boy, did it take me out! I would go on to eventually become numb, and I began to go through the motions. As the corporate politics and negative customers and staff I worked with day in and day out began to really take its toll on my sanity, I would often find solace in a beer or two every evening as a brief escape from the prison to which I had surrendered. I'm sure a few of you can relate here.

The Exit Strategy Takes Root

While serving my "life-sentence" at my college-earned dream job, and constantly convincing myself that things would get better, my new wife, Sam had become a personal trainer at a local big box gym. Fitness and nutrition had radically transformed her life, therefore it wasn't a surprise that she would soon gain a great following of loyal clients. Around this time, I eventually came to the realization that the corporate thing was not for me. It was not what I thought it would be. I was destined for more and being confined to corporate rules and structure was no longer enticing.

As I began to speak with others who were in other corporate fields, I confirmed what I thought to be true; most were equally unsatisfied, but had somehow convinced themselves that this is as good as it gets. Have you ever convinced yourself of this, too?

You reach the point where you are going through the motions. All passion is removed from your day. We were all essentially doing just enough not to get fired, and they were paying us just enough so we would not quit. The difference was that something inside me could not accept "this is as good as it gets." Despite having everyone around me hyping me up about how great the benefits were—the security, the vacations, yadda yadda yadda—deep down, I just knew there had to be more.

I do realize now that their intentions were to prevent me from going into uncharted waters of uncertainty. That fear is what prevents most people from stepping out and becoming more. I don't know, maybe it was because my grandparents, Harold and Shirley, had an entrepreneurial bone, but had failed at a few things. That thought would be a double-edged sword, because on one side, it illustrated hope for more, but on the other side, it reinforced why I should keep my head down and simply accept what I had. And that little doubt would find its opening, and fear crept in to do what it does best—which is to keep you stuck in mediocrity with everyone else; to play it safe and take what life simply throws at you.

Well, I'm happy to say that I decided to stay in the fight. I guess that entrepreneurial gene was passed down. And just maybe I, like my grandparents, were too stubborn to give in to a life of mediocrity. It was a pill that was too hard for me to swallow, so I never did. I would continue to work on ideas of how to grow outside that "job." I was always searching for that "side hustle" to earn a little extra money so I could gain back a little extra time. Maybe you have done the same?

I always found myself discussing with Sam business opportunities in real-estate, small business ideas, you name it. I began reading and listening to personal development books and CDs.

My father-in-law would actually turn me on to a book titled, *The Richest Man in Babylon*. This book would spark a thirst for personal development that would never be quenched to this very day. With every book, I grew one percent better, more confident, and more hopeful of breaking the chains. However, in the meantime, I was giving away the one thing I said I valued the most, and that was more of my time. This led me to becoming more incongruent with what I said I valued.

Eureka! It wasn't about the money, per se; it was about what more "smart" money could provide me. Smart money is money where you are not trading time for dollars. In the right space and business model, more money could create more opportunity and more time freedom. That is what I was searching for! Maybe that is what you, too, are searching for? I just so happened to be looking in all the wrong places, and perhaps you have been, too.

Well, I wish this is where I could say we embarked into creating our direct sales empire, but not so much. This is where we would jump out of the frying pan and into the fire. But all these experiences were lessons to get us where we are today.

We jumped out of being employees to—quite frankly—owning a job. Yep, we created and started our own personal training studio. And to be honest, we would find that we were much happier grinding and pursuing our dreams as opposed to building someone else's dream. Sound familiar?

But we would still find ourselves once again fighting a fight we could not win, as Sam so graciously explained in previous chapters. No matter how we would structure it, or could have structured it, that business model simply could never give us what we wanted to create. Could we have done things differently and impacted a few more lives while enhancing our lives? Possibly, but ultimately we would hit a lid or a ceiling that would prove to be unbreakable. Have you ever felt that way?

We could not get out of our heads that we were built for so much more. We were built to impact not hundreds or even thousands of lives in our community. We were made to impact tens or even hundreds of thousands of lives across the country. And not just in promoting healthy bodies, but in healthy relationships and finances as well. We were designed by God to radically transform our meager lives to a level that shined so bright that it could lead the masses who were also desiring to do more. They just didn't know how.

Choose Your Hard

We were taught to play the "go to college, earn a degree, get your dream job and live happily ever after" card . . . Wait, isn't that the way it's supposed to go? Maybe for some of you, the stars aligned, and that happened; but for most of us, not so much. On the contrary, as most of us would find ourselves going to college, going into student loan debt so we can earn and buy a degree, later to come out of college with no experience, only to get an entry-level job where we could gain work experience while earning enough money to pay back our debt from college for that entry-level position that we hope turns into your dream job that leads us to happily ever after . . .

Look,

- I've experienced college. Yep, been there, done that, and got the degree hanging on the wall to prove it . . .
- I've worked seven years for a Fortune 400 company out of college. Yep, been there, done that, and thankfully, got out before the golden handcuffs imprisoned me . . .
- I've earned back-to-back highest sales awards for the same company. Got the paychecks and trips to prove it . . .

- I've also created and managed our own small business. Yep, been there, done that one, too, and accumulated the debt and stress that went along with it . . .
- Earned the six-figure income (AKA $8,333+ monthly) as gym owners in our twenties . . .

But none of them could lead us to freedom. Ah, that word, "freedom." Just the sound of that word brings peace over me when I say it out loud. I see now why I was so uneasy in all of my careers. I was missing that one thing. Perhaps, you are, too. Freedom from a commute. Freedom from a boss. Freedom from a set schedule. Freedom from capped earnings. Freedom for how many days I could have off. Freedom to be creative. Freedom to take a sick day. Freedom to do what I wanted to do when I wanted to do it. Freedom to go to my kids' school and read a story. Freedom to be the only dad at school field trips.

You see, all of these former jobs and careers would come with their limitations in time, security, purpose, and fortune. Do you agree?

Finding Freedom

We would eventually find our freedom through network marketing. Gone are the days of lying in bed at 2 a.m. wondering:

How am I going to pay this bill?

How am I going to replace this employee?

Am I letting my family down?

How do I get us out of this situation?

What if I take money from this account and move it to this account?

What the hell am I going to do?

I can cut off the cable and put an antenna in the attic, but what else?

When I tell you I would spend so much mental energy on crunching numbers that my compulsive thinking would consume my entire day and eventually my life, I mean that with complete sincerity. I can recall going grocery shopping and always having a second credit card ready to swipe in case the first one would be declined. I would also have the same script prepared if that happened, "Ooops! I'm sorry I gave you the wrong card. That account was closed." This had become my life, and I would be naïve to think that no one else could relate to this at some capacity. This is no way to live a life—in fear, constant struggle, hopeless, and losing joy. I'm telling you now it is no way to live, and you don't have to.

I look back today, just three years later, and can't help but think how much has drastically changed in such a short time. It can for you, too. What seemed like an eternity because of the amount of pain we were in, really was just a vapor of time. To think had we given in to the self-doubt, the fear, the obstacles, the constant resistance. Would our life today just be like another replaying episode? Just that thought reminds me of the movie, *Groundhog Day*. Or if we are being real here, more like *insanity*.

We would later realize that the closer we would get to a new breakthrough, the stronger the resistance would become. It would show up in different ways, too. Sometimes, the resistance would be something breaking at our home, a client quitting, someone becoming ill, or even worse. When we learned to recognize many of these as signs that we were onto something, we became more energized and excited for what was around the corner. And sometimes, the resistance was simply life showing up at an inconvenient time. It was just our current life situation—not our life.

Instead, we chose to focus on what we desired to create. Because to resist and fight against these situations is to resist life. And life always wins.

Today, we simply laugh; sometimes we even embrace resistance and obstacles, especially when we are working on a big project. It is what it is, right? The situation is the situation, and if you don't like it, make a move to change it. Don't label it, judge it, or loathe it. Accept the circumstances and make adjustments to create the situation you desire. That's right; there is a testimony to how much your life can transform in just a few years.

We continue to plug into mentorship via people, books, videos, and podcasts. We continue to allow our best versions to shine through. And I implore you to do the same!

Today, I contend for the dads who desire to be better fathers. Maybe that's you? I contend for the husbands who desire to be better lovers and friends to their wives. I contend for men's masculinity. In a culture where it's socially acceptable and cute to demasculinize men; I contend that it's perfectly normal for a man to be assertive, aggressive, and protective.

All these traits and more are perfectly fine if they are acting from a place of love, respect, and higher consciousness. In fact, I believe they are important for a healthy balance in relationships and society as a whole. Choose your hard, they say. I choose to contend for you and to assist you to revealing your full potential. So you can better serve your family, yourself, and the world.

Get Your Team on Board

No, not your direct sales team, but your family. One of the most important things you can do, aside from getting clear on your "why" and choosing a direct sales company that aligns with your values and goals, is to bring your household in on the plan.

As you commit to turning this #sidehustle or Plan B into something grander, it's going to require you to take your spare time and commit it to growing this new business. Your family will potentially see it as a hindrance, nuisance, or even a threat. They could view it as a distraction. Regardless, you must know in your mind why you are doing this and remember also that they are not mind readers.

Sometimes, in the beginning, we are fighting for people while we also fight against them. Remember, "People will judge you by your actions; not by your intentions." This last phrase from the book, *The Speed of Trust,* was a game-changer in how I approached this situation and many others to this day. I encourage you to do the same and see how its power can radically and positively change your relationships.

Now, what if you don't get them on board? For some of

you, this includes not only your spouse but also your children. Take this as an opportunity to become clearer on what it is you all want to achieve as a family. Have fun with it. Throw all your dreams and desires on the table and talk about the possibilities. Help paint the picture for them that this is the vehicle to deliver on those goals. Let them know that Plan A is providing what you currently have, but if you want more, it's going to take a more capable and robust vehicle to take you there.

It's not just about money, but also about what money can do for your family. What is important to your family is more time with you, having adventures, and doing things you all love to do together (which takes more money or time or both). And with that being said, it's going to require some early sacrifices. Ultimately, it comes down to if you really do desire change, then you are going to need to change a few things.

Take this opportunity to really get their buy-in as part of the team, maybe even by assigning some tasks they can do to contribute to this team goal. It may be chores at dinnertime, or assisting with setting up for local events you host at your home. Whatever it may be, just get them involved if you can. Or maybe it's just asking if they step up a little more on the house chores while you pivot and funnel to getting this new venture up and running. While doing this, set goals with rewards as a family. Setting milestones accompanied with rewards that everyone can share in, is a powerful and tangible thing.

We did this as often as we could, and our kids would be so excited when we would hit a new milestone. When we were in the phase of living on a very tight budget, this often just meant a family picnic to our favorite park. The free or inexpensive celebrations were important. They brought us closer, gave us rest, and helped us dream to the next level. We valued any and all extra time together and every victory became *our* victory as a family.

We included the girls and thanked them for contributing and their support. Yes, even if they were only four and seven years old at the time. Teaching them to be understanding and supportive when we were on late meetings and calls was a game-changer. They were so kind and eager to be a part of this journey with us in any way they could.

I can recall, in 2016, when we took a seventeen-day vacation across the country with not much of a plan, but only that we had the time, money, freedom to just GO! And boy, did we go. We traveled over four-thousand miles in those seventeen days. We lived four days here and there and had some amazing experiences. This vacation right here really put a stamp in our family's minds that, "Hey, all the hard work is really paying off," even if we did have to remind the kids from time to time of why and how we were able to do what we were doing. As you can see, getting the team's buy-in gave not only the family a piece of mind but gave us all more hope and clarity on what we were all contending for which was *freedom*.

Through it all, as we worked to build a life we could live together in full time and financial flexibility, we first became closer in our hearts, because we were united on a common mission. Our children knew that we, as their parents, craved more than anything to build our life around our family.

I would be remiss to not mention my mom here, Diana Schmidt Prestenbach, as one of the key people in our team and family. My mother nurtured and encouraged me my whole life. That did not end just because I grew up and got married. She was our one person that we could turn to and trust our children with. When we needed help at our former brick-and-mortar business, she was there to fill in wherever she could. She was our right-hand woman and worked as much as she could for as little payment as possible to just help us get through to the better days we envisioned. When times were good, we all enjoyed the fruits. When times were bad, we all went without. Most importantly, though I know it was hard for her to see like we saw in our minds, she still believed in us and even while she herself went through some very devastating life changes. Mom, I love you and thank you for everything! You're a part of our adventure.

A Little Taste is All it Takes . . .

Yeah, buddy . . . That moment when what you have been dreaming about for years becomes a reality. Even if it is just a small portion of that dream. Yes, indeed. That, my friend, is the most surreal moment anyone can ever have the privilege to experience. I literally just got goosebumps as I relived that feeling in my head when we experienced our first glimpse and taste of time, location, and financial freedom. Not to mention the joy and peace it brings with it. To this day, I find the time to routinely stop and take a moment to be grateful for the life we contended for and that God, with all His love and grace, gave increase to our life.

I find myself often encouraging our team about "just getting that win" and assisting others to get a win. Why? Because a taste of any victory, big or small, and as often as possible, can become contagious. It can also continue to help motivate and prove to yourself that you're on the right path. Too often, you may underestimate the power in striving and celebrating these small victories. Sam and I utilized these small wins as if they were stepping stones toward the bigger and grander goals we finally arrived at today. Without doing that, I'm not sure we would have made it. I truly believe you can become burned out if you don't slow down to celebrate the many milestones along the way. Now, there will also be times when those bigger victories are further and fewer between. Because bigger goals can take longer to develop sometimes. And this is where it's even more crucial and important to celebrate your actions on a weekly or monthly basis. Big or small, as long as you are knocking them out on a consistent basis then, by all means, take the time to celebrate.

Seriously, it could be as simple as a little jig with the family. That's right, we have had many of celebratory dance parties in the Freedom Parents living room. This is a great example of enjoying the journey while bringing the family in to celebrate together. Being intentional in celebrating these victories helps to create a more joyous journey toward the Freedom Life. Because, let's face it, what you are attempting to create is going to take work; it's going to force you to grow, and it's going to take a little grit. Okay, maybe a lot of grit. But that's what makes the destination that much more rewarding.

In September 2018, we took our first trip back home to Louisiana after our move to Arizona. Upon that homecoming, our first priority was to visit my grandmother, Shirley. This woman is one of the hardest working women I will ever know. Sometimes, we forget to look at our loved ones who came before us to see just how much they worked to elevate their family. MawMaw Shirley and PawPaw Harold (God rest his soul) were looking for more, too. My grandfather was illiterate, but he did not let that stop him either. Together, they both tried their hand at a network marketing company, an emu farm, and a daycare center. My grandfather was a construction worker, but had a vision of getting out of the dirt. He always said, "I have no choice, but you can be better than me." Shirley was tired of starving. She had baby siblings that were going hungry, and so she went to work at a young age to help her mother and father provide. As an adult, she vowed that her family would never know what it would be like to go hungry. So she, too, busted her butt to elevate her family. Their legacy was as great as any other; well-fed children with clothes on their backs, food in their bellies, and a roof over their heads. That is pure grit, and look at the grace that followed in their path.

To create freedom in your health and wealth and to be able to pass that on to others is priceless. To break the chains of mediocrity and show others that they, too, have the choice to do the same if they make the decision; I don't think there is a word that would accurately sum up that amount of epicness.

I jokingly say to a few people I mentor that, "I selfishly desire to help them create freedom, so I have someone to play with during the week." Because, let's face it, everyone else is working during the week with no flexibility in their schedules. On the contrary, to be a #freedomparent is not asking to be off, working for the weekend, or a yearly vacation. Rather, it means to prioritize your life around what matters most to you and your family. It's going horseback riding on a Friday morning with your kids before you start school lessons. It's swimming lessons on a Wednesday morning because evenings or weekends are not ideal for us. It's taking the family on a morning hike during the week before school because we can. Or it's packing up last minute for a trip to wherever because we can. We became #TheFreedomParents for a reason.

I encourage you now to create your "because I can" list. I pray you don't stop until it's a reality.

If you take anything away from this book, I hope it's at least that you have a choice to break away from mediocrity; that you have a choice to start thriving instead of just surviving. And most importantly, I hope you come to realize that your past or current circumstances don't have to define you or your future. I hope you learn to contend for your why because it is so worth it. You're invited to come live free with us and the whole #freedomparenttribe.

Are you ready?

The Freedom Parent Playlist

You can also find this playlist on Spotify and iTunes.

1. Fast Car - Tracy Chapman
2. Keep Your Eyes Open - NEEDTOBREATHE
3. Cough Syrup - Young the Giant
4. Under Pressure - Queen & David Bowie (or, My Chemical Romance)
5. For The First Time - The Script
6. Nothing Left To Lose - Mat Kearney
7. Walk - The Foo Fighters
8. Wheels - Foo Fighters
9. Try - Pink
10. I Will Wait- Mumford & Sons
11. Made For You- One Republic
12. Counting Stars - One Republic
13. Secrets - One Republic
14. On Top Of The World - Imagine Dragons

15. You Get What You Give - New Radicals

16. Brother - NEEDTOBREATHE

17. Home - Phillip Phillips

18. This Is Me- The Greatest Showman Soundtrack

19. In The Light - The Lumineers

20. High Hopes - Panic! At the Disco

21. Sign Me Up - Matt Hartke

22. Just Breathe - Pearl Jam

23. You and Me - Dave Matthews Band

24. Keep Your Head Up - Andy Grammer

25. My Body - Young the Giant

26. Whatever It Takes - Imagine Dragons

27. Thunder - Imagine Dragons

28. Believer - Imagine Dragons

29. It's Time - Imagine Dragons

30. Good Life - One Republic

31. Feel Again - One Republic

32. A Million Dreams - The Greatest Showman Soundtrack

33. Come Alive - The Greatest Showman Soundtrack

34. The Greatest Show - The Greatest Showman Soundtrack

35. Here Comes the Sun - The Beatles

The #FreedomParentTribe Tells You About Their New American Dream

Robert and Laura Gaffney

We are Laura and Bob Gaffney. Our journey started when I decided to try this program as I desperately needed to lose some weight. Bob and I were also searching eagerly for a profit center to add to our small business; we own a fitness center, Pulse Health and Fitness Club, in Maryland, and even after thirteen years, we did not have a viable solution for our members who wanted to lose weight (obviously, this was true as even I could not figure out how to get into better health myself).

Accepting that exercise is not the answer to fat-loss, we were delighted to find a way to give our members what they needed; improved health while developing an awesome profit center. I lost forty pounds, but I gained so much more! Personally, I wasn't feeling fulfilled in my life.

As a recovering alcoholic with five years sobriety, I yearned for a community of like-minded healthy and vibrant people. I have found this community and so much more and am a happier person all around! This has been such a blessing.

For Bob, as a small business owner, he was feeling unfulfilled as he felt limited in his ability to impact other people's lives. Now, with this amazing tool, he is able to not only help local people but also people around the globe. As business mentors, we are also able to offer the gift of financial freedom to anyone who dares to dream the American Dream. Coaching for just a little over two years now, we are already seeing the huge financial opportunity that awaits us! Our dream is to assist as many people around the world as we can to physical, personal, and financial health while creating time for each other and our family and to eventually be able to leave a great legacy.

Allen and Maria Fernandez

Hi, my name is Maria. I started my little side hobby five years ago as a stay-at-home mom. I was married to an offshore crane mechanic, in a new town, with two small babies. I was an inspired and empowered person, yet also bored and lonely. I had recently lost a hundred pounds, and I realized helping others held me accountable.

So, I started my then #sidehustle because it gave me a platform to leave an impact, interact with other adults and have something fun to do between changing diapers. To my surprise, I soon had plenty of purpose, passion, and extra shopping money. I was hot. I was healthy. I was happy . . .

But I looked at my husband, and he was not. He was (at the time) working twenty-seven days out of the month on an oil rig. He was being shipped off to foreign countries while leaving crying babies behind to be nothing more than a number on a job site. He soon would feel the chaos of the industry, when a 2016 recession left him sitting at home with only half the paycheck of the previous years. He was broken and beat up at the time, yet my heart was thrilled to have him home. He may have been just an employee out there, but in our home, he was irreplaceable.

His presence gave me peace, leadership, confidence . . . he gave our children direction, support and stability. I looked at the opportunity in my hands and realized I had the key to keeping him home permanently.

I never wanted to see crying kids in the back of my car after dropping daddy off at the airport again. I felt compelled to use the blueprint set before me and end the chaos of our family being separated. I started helping others at a higher level because I was determined. We all worked together that year, and in February of 2018, he walked away from the oil industry completely!

He is now home fulfilling a role only he can fill. He provides peace, stability, and adventure to our lives. As a family, we've changed everything. Our kids tend school virtually as we travel the country full time. Our children see the fruits of our efforts daily. They see us pour into our coaches, but then they also see us turn it all off to play with them and be present at the end of the day.

We have completely broken the mold of the American dream, and we're not sorry at all! In fact, it has propelled others to realize they, too, can chase their dreams! We've lived our best lives this past year, but we now know what we hold is no longer just for us! It's for giving away!

So this year as we focus, pray and reflect . . . we're thrilled to see the blessing unfold in the lives around us. We are excited to follow the direction of our hearts. We are excited to hold an amazing gift for those who are brought into our life. We are compelled to bring freedom to other families who feel stuck like we once did, and we are excited to see what that freedom will mean for them.

Jared and Megan Braud

As we began our lives together, we both knew we wanted to start a family and give so much to our children. I always wanted to be a stay-at-home mom and wife, and I told my husband that from the beginning. I was working in ministry at the time and felt great about what I was contributing to the care of others, but I was not feeling as though this was truly fulfilling to me.

Jared knew I wanted to be home with our future children, whenever that may be, but deep down, he had strong doubts it could ever happen. Being the one who does our finances, he knew where we stood as far as needing my income and there was no light at the end of that tunnel as far as he could see. So we continued on, knowing that dream was there, but in dreamland . . . where we both knew it would stay.

Once the opportunity was presented to us to become entrepreneurs, we decided to start dreaming a little closer to our hearts . . . still not close enough, though. The dream started to look a little less blurry but the figure of how it would shape out still wasn't clear. But for us, dreaming was a good start.

It wasn't long after I came home to run our business that

we found out we were starting our family . . . with TWINS! This hit Jared's financial gut pretty hard. Within the first six months of having our girls, our finances hit a scary deep slope. He began to stress over making ends meet. He even avoided talking with me about our finances. That only caused frustration between the two of us.

I was watching my husband get swallowed in his anxiety. It hurt to see him wake up every morning with a knot in the pit of his stomach. He would go off to work, and we would be praying for a raise he hadn't seen in over five years.

It was *this* moment I realized I had the key in my hand . . . what was I waiting for? Was I going to sit around and sulk, allowing our family to drown in anxiety and stress? Or was I going to put my big-girl panties on and fight for our freedom to not just dream a dream, but to live the dream?

We saw the shift in our attitudes make a shift in our freedom and in our back account. Our dreams became a reality! Not only did our dream come true, and I became a work-from-home-mom of two beautiful twin girls, but my husband has been relieved of the crippling grasp that lack of money once held him in. We don't allow our dreams to be small . . . we make our dreams bigger than we can imagine. We now have the freedom to dream bigger than ever . . . so we dream freely!

Trey and Leslie Begin

In the Fall of 2013, I was a stay-at-home mom of four sweet girls who felt trapped in the mundane, less than satisfied with my current reality. I loved my girls, but I was forty-five pounds overweight, tired, and lacked enthusiasm in all areas of my life. I reached out to a friend, and she offered me an opportunity to get healthy physically. One healthy change led to another, and once I lost some weight, I believed that *anything* was possible. I started taking risks in life. I started to help and serve others well. My life started to take on new meaning as I lived a life of inspiration, created healthy community, and our finances started getting better.

One night, I found my thirty-four-year-old husband laying on our bed convinced he was having a heart attack. The pressure of providing for our growing family and the families of all the other employees we had in our other business was such a heavy burden for him to emotionally and mentally carry. At the hospital, sitting in the emergency room, we learned that he had a panic attack and not a heart attack. As I watched him laying in the bed attached to the different machines, I realized that something needed to change. We longed for a different life, and we were willing to work for the change we needed to see.

In the process of the work, I became a better mommy. I was engaged, fun, and excited to be a parent. I became a flirty and fun wife. I started to grow into the best version of myself. As I grew, my husband grew. There were some massive roadblocks along the way but we really saw that facing the obstacles instead of running from them would allow us to learn from them. There were some heartbreaks along the way as well, and we decided to persist and take action even in the midst of these. And our family grew by two additional little girls along the way, each new birth compelled us to take uncommon action. This persistence and consistent action grew into a new freedom in our lives financially, mentally, emotionally, physically, and spiritually. We were growing, expanding, and being refined.

Now the future is bright. Our six girls are living a life where their parents bring them to school and pick them up from school. They have parents who are not stressed and exhausted, but instead, are awakened, alive, and interested in them. Our home is characterized by laughter and fun. What once seemed absolutely impossible now seems probable! The options in our life are literally limitless. We can live anywhere we want to live. We can give as generously as we want to give. We can live as big as we have been called to live. We are living as a part of the #thefreedomparents movement!

Allen and Elizabeth Heil

I have known Sam and Harold for over ten years now. I remember being one of their first clients at Lift, their old business/life. Samantha and I immediately clicked, and I think I worked out as much as possible just to spend time with her. She had a way of talking to me that I have never responded to before. If she said run two miles today, I did it! Who was this person . . . meaning her and myself? I literally ran my first 5k race within two months of training with her. I had the joy of getting to know her and her family as I watched her bring her first daughter into the world while owning a gym. I can remember Sabella in her infant seat while Sam trained me. I truly had the joy of watching this amazing couple transform not only their lives, bodies, and finances, but their family as well.

Samantha asked me to join her coaching family more times than I can count for over two years. At those times, I was just too busy and easily overwhelmed with life. It wasn't until I was a client again and I filled out a well-being evaluation that I got serious.

Sam was floored to find out that me, a business owner with two incomes, was in very poor financial shape.

But it happens and can happen to the best of us. She reached out and invited me to coffee, and when I looked into her eyes and saw her genuine concern about me, my stressed-out life, working three jobs, and owning a business, I knew I had to finally listen to her and allow myself to be open to joining this mission. So I jumped in that day. Allen and I had lunch with them the very next day and purchased our kit on a credit card and a prayer.

I had always trusted Sam, and I knew this was the path for me. Before this day, we were stressed beyond stressed. I was working three jobs and had two girls in college. We had made some poor financial decisions over the years and desperately needed help.

We were hopeless at this point and literally just surviving from day to day.

Allen, my husband, was even more distraught and very depressed. He had shared with me that he had contemplated suicide on more than one occasion due to our situation. This is when I knew we had to do something to make some serious changes, and luckily, the Prestenbachs were there when we needed them most.

We had recently sold our home that we built twelve years prior. The same home we had purposefully filled with so much love and raised our amazing daughters in was gone. But we did what we had to do to make matters better. Moving forty miles east to Mississippi to help our financial situation was one thing we could do even though I didn't want to leave my home. I was doing okay on my own personal journey but needed some accountability.

Within about three months of following the Prestenbach's lead and the systems in place, we were seeing the rewards of this amazing gift they had given us. I was able to quit my first part-time job as a nanny by May, and by the end of the summer, I was financially able to quit my second job but decided to go back for another school year.

This opportunity allowed us to breathe financially for the first time in years, and we both had hope again.

We were finally *dreaming* again about our future instead of dreading it and our relationship was thriving again as well. In August of 2018, I made the decision not to return to my job so I could stay at home (or wherever I want to work) and work my new business full time!

It has been amazing reaping the rewards of true freedom. I can work my business from anywhere, travel with my husband, visit my daughter 2,000 miles away, help my family when needs arrive—like babysitting etc. Even though a lot of my family/friends just didn't understand, why would I quit doing something I loved—counseling—and recently went to graduate school for? Well, times were changing and mental health is at it's all-time worst in Louisiana and everywhere in the country.

I loved my job, but I was stressed, and my days were spent dealing with crisis after crisis instead of actual counseling. I had to be willing to give up the *good* for *great,* and I am so glad I did. I get to do literally whatever I want from wherever I want daily. Who would not want this amazing life that we have now created? Yes, we are empty-nesters, but we still get to dream and have goals and see ourselves doing this until we die and enjoy being the most awesome grandparents while traveling the world and not being tied down to office walls! That's our New American Dream!

Stephanie Robbins

I met Sam, and eventually Harold, about two years ago through Facebook. Sam's tenacity, determination, and wisdom was so inspiring. At the time, I was a stay-at-home mom with two beautiful kids. I have to say, at this time in my life, although from all outward appearances looked victorious, I was actually very broken on the inside.

You see, I had become an extreme introvert, lacking self-confidence, and I felt like I didn't really belong anywhere. We were stable financially, but my husband worked several jobs in order to provide extra income that would allow us to travel and make memories with our kids. All my friends and family thought I was so strong, but caring for two children with cystic fibrosis was taking a mental toll on me.

Sam was such a light at that time, showing me through social media what it looked like to be strong, self-confident, and empowered. I knew I wanted what she had. We talked back and forth for six months while I let fear paralyze me from moving forward toward my own freedom. Then finally something had to give. I knew I was meant for more, and I knew Sam and Harold held the key. So I finally set aside my fears and jumped in with both feet. It started out as a way to belong to an amazing community of positive people, but quickly became so much bigger.

You see, once my husband was also diagnosed with cystic fibrosis, I knew right then and there that God had put Sam in my path for a reason. This was what I was meant to do, and it was the vehicle to provide true freedom in finances, but more importantly, time. Time with my family, the people I love, when I know that time may be limited. I now have the freedom to make sure we make the most of the time we are given.

I am now well on my way to bringing my husband home from his now only job, paving the way for us to be truly free to spend the time we have left together. What started out as a way for me to find myself again has turned into freedom beyond what I ever thought possible.

Sarah Franatovich

Hi! My name is Sarah, and I am a Freedom Parent!

If you would have shown me a picture of who I am today a year ago, I wouldn't have believed this transformation was possible. Sure, the ninety-four pounds I lost makes me look really different (awesome) in the mirror, but there is more than that. Today, I am different. I am changed. I am a new person.

A year ago, there was nothing really wrong with my life. I would wake up every day, go to work, take care of the kids, and have all the different things going on at night with the children. I was fine! Just living a mundane life, day in and day out doing the same thing over and over. You know, doing whatever was on the schedule for the day. And then I embarked on this journey. A journey I wasn't even looking for; a side-hustle, per se, that I didn't even really need (or so I thought).

At the beginning, I was asked to dream a little. What do you want in life? What are some big things that you love? I couldn't even really come up with much. It was hard for me to dream. I was just stuck in a spot of a mundane life, and I couldn't picture anything else existing. But I embarked on the journey, anyway. I wanted to help people around me go through what I went through. And what I found is that now I am full of life and full of joy! My dream was to insert excitement into my life.

I have a new reason and a purpose to live. I thought I had purpose before, but it is totally different now. It's difficult to explain unless you have experienced it, but the idea of helping people see who they really are, showing them they have purpose, too, and helping them get outside of the stinking thinking in their heads to understand that there is so much more to life and so much more to give—*that* is so amazing.

Freedom for me is simply helping others become free from the everyday shackles that restrain them from being great.

The purpose I have now and the drive that I have to be able to do that for myself and others (knowing that my story inspires people) is beyond belief for me. I think, in the past, I was just another person walking along the path of life, but now, I feel like I stand out.

I feel like people look at me, and they are inspired by me, by my story and by my life. When I walk into a room, people feel different. And that is because of this journey I embarked on. That is because I chose freedom for myself first. I decided this was the time for me to do something different.

I still work a full-time job, because for me, I love to have both my career as a CPA and my passion of being an entrepreneur and HOPE dealer. I do this side hustle literally in the nooks and crannies of anything I can possibly pull off throughout the day.

If I am in the car, I am on the phone. If I am in between meetings, I am making things happen. I don't waste time. I prioritize everything I need to do. And I make sure it all works out because I realize how important this is not only to my journey and my accountability in my life, but also to help the people around me. Because they deserve what I received through this process and this journey that I've embarked on. I am super excited, and I hope that if nothing else, you are encouraged today.

Encouraged to do something different. That you are encouraged to step out of your comfort zone and make yourself realize there is something bigger, there is something more and you *can* have it! Start to dream like I have and watch your life flood with joy and excitement. You might even break up the monotony of life to realize you can live an unscripted life.

Patrick Hunter and Miriam Hunter

Our story really begins with me, Miriam. I had always dreamed of being a mother and had always dreamed of staying at home with my kids. That's what we were doing. That is the dream we were living. However, the reality of that dream was very different for me as I was living it out in real time.

After having two babies sixteen and a half months apart, I struggled terribly with postpartum depression and anxiety. I would dread getting out of bed each day. I looked at my two precious children, the children that we had hoped and prayed for, and what I felt was joy and despair all at the same time. I did not know who I was anymore. I felt like I didn't know who "Miriam" was. I had lost my hope and my spark for life, and I didn't realize how deep my fear went.

That is what our life looked like. We thought we were living our dream, and that things were as good as they could get, but in reality, it was mostly fear and anxiety captivating our existence. My husband, Patrick, works as a special education teacher and a coach and had the pressure of earning the only income for our family. Yes, he loves his job, but we were pinching pennies and agonizing over every dollar spent.

We sat down in December of 2017 and looked at our bills, and we were faced with the reality that what we were doing was not working, and that we could not go on.

In the midst of teaching and coaching two sports, Patrick and I decided that he should apply for another degree program so that he could earn more income for our family.

That was when we were given a glimpse of hope and freedom . . . we didn't really know the freedom that was possible for us, but I saw a friend who was living a more free life. I trusted her that the freedom was there, and so I followed her down the path of entrepreneurship because I believed in what she was doing to help other people.

I honestly never thought of myself as an entrepreneur or a businesswoman. I *never* thought I would run my own business, but my ability to run my own business has given me hope again. It has helped me to find "who I am."

I had someone tell me once, "Become who you are." What

he meant was: work to become the person you were made to be. And I had lost sight of that. Throughout my life, I was always the bubbly, joyful one who was the life of the party, but I had withdrawn from life. People had no idea what was going on inside of me because I put on a smile for the world while, in reality, I had such hurt and brokenness in my heart.

Now we live in a place of hope, freedom, and abundance. The ability to grow and work alongside other people as we help give them hope has forced me to grow as a person. It has pushed me to grow in ways that I would not have otherwise. As an entrepreneur, I have been allowed to see that I can do more than what I could have ever dreamed . . . I am a #Mom-Boss! Who knew that my soul just needed a little more? Who knew that I could handle more, but "more" was just the answer.

This process has transformed our marriage: My husband did not feel like he was married to the woman he dated and married. He felt like the real Miriam was held captive. He was fearful of what might happen if we stepped out and did something that scared us. It was hard to step out of that scarcity mindset into the abundance mindset.

Now, our children have a mamma who is home with them and has the ability to work from anywhere at any time that I choose. I can hold a sick baby on my hip while I am working from my phone. My husband has the ability to do the teaching and coaching job that he loves without the pressure of having to get extra degrees that he has no interest in. Our side hustle has benefitted not just our family and our marriage, but now we have the ability offer hope and freedom to others who don't think that they can find it.

We are creating an atmosphere in our home where we hope that our children will thrive and that our family will be seen as a family that gives joy and hope to others. We strive to be authentic, genuine, honest, and open. In this way people might look at the life we are creating and say, "Gosh! If they can come from what they came from, and they can do it, maybe we can, too!?!" Because that is the way we started. So we hope this will inspire some hope and some joy!

Today, we are the people, and are still *becoming* the people, that we were made to be and we know that you can, too!

Johnny Schmidt

I met Harold when we were in college together at Southeastern Louisiana University. We shared some of the same business classes for the last two years of our college careers. Although, I didn't know him well, we seemed to have a connection that lead to mutual respect and friendship quickly.

We went our separate ways after graduation, like most do, but I began to see him on Facebook around 2016. I had been grinding it out in the corporate world since graduating college in 2003 and had been moving from one job to another looking for something that truly filled my heart.

I could never find anything that gave me what I was so desperately looking for: a sense of purpose, meaning, and true fulfillment.

I kept trying different side gigs to help with my finances, but I never found anything that I really believed in; the passion wasn't there. That makes it really hard to succeed when you don't really care about what you're doing. Working for bosses who only see you as a number, rather than a person with goals and aspirations, will only motivate you to work just hard enough not to get fired and keep payday coming.

That's no way to live! We are not meant to sit at a computer, in a cubicle, working eight-plus hours a day, just to live paycheck to paycheck. We are not meant to put up with bosses and managers that have your every move under a microscope. People who make you feel like you're only as good as your last week's performance. We are meant for so much more, or at least I was convinced that I had a better destiny waiting.

That's when I began to see Harold on Facebook and I could tell he was making a difference in people's lives, but that he also was enjoying his life, too!

It intrigued me to reach out and find out what he was doing. Although, I thought I was doing well with this medical sales job—earning six figures a year, and having to ask permission to take vacations, etc—I was desperately looking for a way out of the corporate world. I was hoping he could help.

He did exactly that. After speaking with him, I knew that I wanted to live the #Freedompreneur life. I quickly turned this new "side gig" into my permanent gig. For the last five years, I was stuck in medical sales, and now all I know is being a #Freedompreneur.

Thank God I made the leap, because I was laid-off from my job within six months of starting my "side gig." But I can honestly say, with complete and utter confidence, that this was the first time I've been laid-off and was not worried about my future in the slightest bit.

In only six months, I had built and created a business that

not only replaced my income from medical sales, but actually exceeded it!

I no longer have to put up with greedy bosses, micro-managers, or ask permission to take vacations or days off. My life is one big vacation all the time, simply doing work I love from wherever I choose.

I no longer have to punch a clock, or get to the office on time driving through traffic every day. I no longer have to trade my time for money. I am no longer building someone else's future and dreams. I am now building my own future. I am now doing something that brings me purpose. I am now doing something that brings me meaning. I am now doing something that brings me fulfillment. I am doing something I believe in, and I am passionate about, and it's all because it changed my life.

It changed my life by helping me lose thirty-five pounds and getting me to my healthy target weight. I became more confident and developed a positive attitude. I grow every day. Now I seek and crave personal development. It was an element that allowed me to get out of the corporate world I so desperately wanted to leave. Finding an opportunity that could actually be an American Dream allowed me to build finances beyond my wildest dreams. But more importantly, this "side gig" has allowed me to offer this amazing gift to friends and family. I am actually creating a life of freedom for others who desire it.

The lives being impacted beyond my own is something I never thought was possible. This has been the most rewarding "job" I've ever had, and I am looking forward to seeing what the future holds for those who choose this life of freedom as I did.

I may not be married right now or have children, but I am still a Freedom Parent! I am offering this gift to those who desire it and giving moms and dads the chance to go home to their families while providing significant incomes. And what's great is that when I do meet that special someone, I will have the time and financial freedom that will allow me to really enjoy the time I have with her, and not have to worry about taking off work or paying bills.

I will be able to give her my time and attention without the added stresses of the corporate grind and finances. I now get to work from anywhere, anytime, and can travel anytime I want to. Who wouldn't want that kind of freedom? I will continue to pursue this life of freedom as long as I live, and I will continue to offer this gift to those who desire it equally as long. This journey will never stop; I have found real freedom.

Dallas and Jessica Mushtare

We were introduced to the Freedom Parent lifestyle when Samantha became one of my business mentors in my new at-home small business of helping people find freedom mentally, physically, and financially. I was in desperate need of all these things for myself and my family, but I had no hope and was in survival mode.

We were broke, broken, and our marriage was failing. We were stuck in mud and spinning our wheels fighting to get out, but going nowhere! I remember walking into my mentor's house for the first time, sitting down with Samantha and my coach Leslie, and immediately having words of life poured into me.

They taught me to dream and to visualize what was possible for me and my family. They ignited hope into me! I remember specifically, this day, Samantha said to me, "You are amazing, you are going to impact so many lives, you are going to make a difference, and you can and will overcome!"

Those powerful words kept me going over the next six months as my family overcame some massive obstacles that were mentally and physically exhausting. There were mornings those words embedded by Samantha into my brain pushed me up out of bed when all I wanted to do was to cry with my head buried under my pillow.

The obstacles kept coming, but we grew stronger! The more obstacles we overcame the stronger we got! We continued to seek out the videos and lives on social media that Sam, Harold, and other Freedom Parents would share. I looked forward to Thursday coffee chats online where Harold would pour life-breathing words into us that gave me even more hope!

Before I knew it, we had transformed from victims of our circumstances and into freedom fighters! Fast forward two and a half years . . . we have gone from surviving to thriving. The chains that were breaking us has turned into *us* becoming chain-breakers!

Through living the Freedom Parent lifestyle, being mentored and poured into by other Freedom Parents who walked before us, we were able to begin to live a life that mattered, a life that inspired others to say, "If they can do it, we can do it."

We were able to break free from heaps of credit-card debt, and I was able to quit the other three jobs I was working. We sold the home we were once under payments in and became financially thriving enough to build our dream freedom home. All at the same time, we healed our marriage, became fun parents again, traveled across the US on a family road trip for the entire summer, and found time-freedom to live a life centered on what mattered most to us!

We no longer live in chains! We have been set free! Now, we live to pass on the gift of being Freedom Parents to as many as we can! I know what it feels like to think there is no possible physical way out when you are so far down and out, but never forget God says you can do all things! Take your first step forward! Every baby step counts, and I assure you, leads you to complete freedom!

57732934R00143

Made in the USA
Columbia, SC
12 May 2019